Passport to Servanthood

Passport to Servanthood

EARL R. MARTIN

BROADMAN PRESS

Nashville, Tennessee

© Copyright 1988 • Broadman Press
All Rights Reserved
4272-32
ISBN: 0-8054-7232-0
Dewey Decimal Classification: B
Subject Heading: MASTON, THOMAS B.
Library of Congress Catalog Number: 87-15333
Printed in the United States of America

Library of Congress Cataloging-in-Publication Data

Martin, Earl R., 1927-
   Passport to servanthood / Earl R. Martin.
      p.   cm.
   ISBN 0-8054-7232-0 : $7.95
   1. Maston, T. B. (Thomas Burford), 1897-   . 2.
Baptists—United States—Clergy—Biography.   3. Southern
Baptist Convention—Clergy—Biography.   4.
Baptists—Missions.   5. Missions—Theory—History of
doctrines—20th century.   I. Title.
BX6495.M362M37 1988
266'.6132'0924—dc 19
[B]   87-15333
                                                CIP

**To Jane,
the great encourager**

Contents

Preface

In the fall of 1985 on the campus of Southwestern Baptist Seminary, regular morning walks with T. B. Maston enhanced my friendship with him immeasurably. We would meet at the corner of the campus and talk as we walked. Greeting students, we would thread our way past the buildings to the seminary post office. After getting our mail I usually accompanied him to his office in the Roberts Library. He works there for an hour or two as often as the weather allows him to get out of the house.

One morning during our walk he told how he had awakened very early with thoughts about the next needed project. He said that he sensed the need for a book about his missionary journeys. I seized on the idea and urged him to write it. It is undoubtedly a story begging to be told. He declined, saying it would be better for someone else to write it. He asked me to help him find someone to write it, assuring that he would cooperate with whomever might be found. After unsuccessfully approaching several prospective authors, it fell to me to make an attempt. This book is the result.

Maston has had a long unofficial career in missions as a professor—both stationary and itinerant. This book is about his remarkable missionary involvement and influence. From the beginning he insisted that the story would include the family—all four of them. I was pleased to comply with his urgent request.

This is not a biography. He has insisted that he does not want anyone to write a book about his life. Nevertheless, it is necessarily biographical. Maston's missionary interest goes back to the time of his conversion and subsequent calling to Christian service. The story begins by giving the background for these experiences. It then traces his pilgrimage in missions through more than seven decades of service among Baptists.

I express my appreciation to Nancy Bedford for her competent assistance in research. She also gave valuable comments as a reader of the manuscript. Others who, likewise, assisted me considerably in reading and research are: T. B. Maston; Mrs. T. B. Maston (Mommie); my wife, Jane; Thurmon Bryant; William M. Pinson; and Bobbie Sorrill. I am also grateful for the solid encouragement from Keith Parks, president of the Southern Baptist Foreign Mission Board, and his staff.

Foreword

This is a new experience for me. This book is concerned with some mission experiences of myself and my family. I have been asked to write a foreword. It is something that I have never done before for a book written by someone else.

Incidentally, my family includes Mrs. Maston, or "Mommie," our elder son, Tom Mac, and our younger son, Eugene or Gene. Tom Mac is seriously handicapped and has lived at home with us for the sixty-one years of his life. He has accompanied us on several of our extended trips overseas. Eugene resides in New York City. He has had some rather distinctive missionary experiences himself.

You will discover that this is not a biography. Rather it is an attempt to concentrate on one phase of the life of our family. After returning from one of our missionary trips I can remember something I said to the first seminary class that I met. I began, "Some of you students are planning after you have finished your training to go to one of our mission fields. My advice to you is not to go if you cannot love people of all colors, classes, and conditions of life."

I want to express my appreciation to Earl Martin, a former student and missionary friend. He has taken time from a busy teaching load at Southwestern Seminary to gather and interpret this material as it relates to our missionary journeys. I would add thanks to those who have cooperated with him in preparing the material. Gratitude is due also to the staff of the Southern Baptist Foreign Mission Board for the encouragement they have given to this project.

Our prayer and hope is that the book will be blessed by our Heavenly Father. May it be used by Him to touch some Christian families to pursue a deeper walk with the Lord. Perhaps that may well lead some of them to embark on missionary journeys of their own.

T. B. Maston
May, 1987

1
Promises to Keep

The last generation of greats born in a log cabin is fading from the American scene. Throughout the history of the United States notable persons like Abraham Lincoln and Sam Houston were born or bred in log cabins. Symbolically, even the log cabin itself has given way to the pre-cut fully modernized vacation cottage.

Among Southern Baptists, however, there is a man who was born in an East Tennessee log cabin at the end of the nineteenth century. His name is Thomas Buford Maston. He is a man of Lincolnesque integrity. Some heroes manifest greatness through military prowess, political fame, genius in the arts, or brilliant oratory. For Maston it is different. He manifests greatness through servanthood.

His birth was humble, similar to the childhood circumstances of other notable Southern Baptists—J. B. Gambrell, George W. Truett, R. G. Lee, and J. M. Dawson. Call his humble entry into the world a passport to servanthood. For God gave him a long-term visa to minister among Baptists through the past six-and-a-half decades of phenomenal growth and painful turmoil. His visa extends to four-score-and-nine years and beyond!

With his passport T. B. Maston has impacted Southern

Baptists in many realms. Baptists have frequently beamed tributes in his direction: inspirer of youth, outstanding professor, friend of students, pioneer of biblical ethics, conscience of Southern Baptists, pathfinder in race relations, renowned denominational servant, prolific author, model churchman, and extraordinary husband and father. There remains at least one more commendation. It sharpens the focus on missions. David Lockard, former student and friend, crowns the list calling him, "Missionary without portfolio." Indeed Maston best magnifies his servanthood in the arena of missions.

Conversion

Young Tom Maston's travel toward the arena of missions inspires the inquiring soul. He awakened to missions on a gradual winding path that led through youth to manhood. His conversion experience launched him on his way. His family gave him an opportune environment for the spiritual journey. The Smithwood community near Knoxville, Tennessee, provided a favorable setting for his experience of grace.

Tom's father was named Samuel Houston Maston. The name expressed the admiration of his parents for the East Tennessee-born hero. By so naming him, they signified their ambition to have a son grow up with the same quality of greatness. They might even have wished that he would become famous. Their son fulfilled the first part of their yearning. Samuel Maston was a man of sterling character. Their grandson completed their hope in ways they might not have dreamed. Tom Maston received the baton of character from his father and carried it to fulfillment in Kingdom service.

Samuel Maston's ancestry derived from his father's Pennsylvania Dutch heritage combined with the Southern Appalachian legacy of both parents. In his youth, he gained an eighth-grade education. He extended it substantially by regular and wide reading. His son pictures him as "a raw-boned hillbilly . . . a man of robust character, deep integrity, and strong will . . . universally respected." Lean and muscular, he worked industriously both on the railroad and in the fields. He taught his children how to work hard and how to play. At home, play became an important agenda for him as the leader of a growing family. He was also a man of genuine Christian conviction.

Samuel married Sarah Sellers, a sixteen-year-old mountaineer's daughter of solid Southern Appalachian stock. From her mother she inherited a dose of French blood. Maston remembers his mother as one "tender in her makeup." She was a modest woman with only a third-grade education. Sarah Maston gave herself devotedly to her family to the point of being quite possessive. Tom cherished her for the loving care she provided. However, her influence on him would always be secondary to that of his father's.

Tom grew up the youngest of three children. Both his sister, Nora, and his brother, "Red," had red hair. Tom's was coal black. During childhood he and "Red" were close. In their teen years differing interests put some distance between them. Tom was timid and unassuming. "Red" was an outgoing and winsome young man with ambitions for a business career. Nora's caring ways left an indelible impression on young Tom. She exerted a considerable influence for good and for Christ.

As a teenager Tom made a striking impression in the small rural community. It was unstudied, to be sure. His height was only five feet eight inches, but he looked taller because of his thick crop of jet-black hair. A brawny body made up for his short stature. Thick muscular arms joined sturdy legs through a solid trunk. It came from hard farm labor. His father saw to that. Maston insists that he was able to hold his own with those who were much bigger. The young athlete amply demonstrated the boast by an impressive record playing football in high school and college. This was so in spite of a childhood injury to his right eye. It left him virtually blind on that side of his face. During his junior year in high school he began wearing eyeglasses for reading. The only adjustment his eye injury required for his participation in sports was in baseball. After a considerable time of playing, he learned that he could do better at the plate if he batted left-handed. His ability to see the ball was effectively improved. His batting average doubled.

The Maston family lived in a sharecropper's house on the Sanders farm. To the west, open country exposed woodland and hills. Eastward stretched the Smithwood community. It consisted of farms and scattered houses focused around a grade school, a corner grocery store, the Baptist church, and the cemetery. The houses were strung out along the highway toward the end of the Knoxville streetcar line. Most of the residents worked in the city.

The Maston house stood at the edge of a wood. It was a stone's throw west of the residence of the landowners, the Sanders family. The tenant's homestead provided room enough for a kitchen garden, a hog pen, and grazing space for a cow or two. It was a mile-and-a-half walk to the Central High School of Fountain City, a suburb on the outskirts of Knoxville.

The building of the Smithwood Baptist Church possessed the customary white-framed construction of the period. It did not betray to strangers that anything of consequence ever happened there. Contrary to appearances it was the hub of activity for the community. The structure provided a shell for the religious life of those of the Baptist persuasion. Inside was a meeting hall with two sections of benches divided by a center aisle. The "ole time religion" prevailed within the four walls. The aisle aimed at the pulpit. Frequently the man behind the pulpit aimed at the occupants of the benches on both sides. It was usually in shotgun fashion. That was the way of mountain preaching. Near the front on either side stood two cast-iron stoves that were fired with coal in fall and winter. But summer or winter the pulpit produced the only fire that really mattered.

As an early teenager, Tom resisted going to the church. His father and sister went regularly. Sarah Maston had joined the congregation. However, embarrassed about her scant education and inability to read, she was unwilling to attend services. Red pursued interests that excluded going to church. Once when Nora wanted someone to accompany her to a Sunday School social she invited her younger brother to go along. Somewhat to her surprise and considerable pleasure, he consented.

The social was a turning point in Tom's life. The Kincaid family provided their home next to the church for the event. Upon entering the living room Tom immediately recognized other teenagers who also attended Central High. Shying away from an empty chair next to some girls from his class, he saw Otey Bryan sitting on the couch. Tom made a beeline for the empty seat next to Otey. He felt more comfortable with a known acquaintance than sitting next to a bunch of giggling girls.

The games began with the standard icebreaker "Animal Hunt." Mrs. Kincaid had prepared slips of paper with the names of various domestic and wild animals. She pinned a slip on the back of every participant. Then she explained that each one had to discover the identity of his or her animal by asking *yes* or *no* questions. Once a player successfully guessed his animal identity someone would transfer the paper from the back to the front of the person. Tom was an elephant but did not know it yet. Shyly mingling around the room from person to person he again tried to avoid the girls. Nevertheless, before long one he had shyly noticed with short brunette hair approached him. Color came to his face as she confronted him. She was clever about asking questions. His responses helped reveal her animal's identity. Still shy, he moved quickly away to safer ground. Darting over to a mature woman in the middle of the room he saw the sign "MULE" pinned on the front of her dress. *How inappropriate,* he thought. Through his line of questioning with her at last it registered that he was the animal with the long snout and longer memory.

Just then Nora appeared. Smilingly she introduced the lady to him as Pearl Sanders, the teacher of the boys' class. Gently Pearl urged him to come to her class in Sunday School. He made a vague promise knowing in his heart he would go the following Sunday. When he mentioned it to Otey they arranged to rendezvous so he would have some reinforcement when he walked into the church building.

The boys' class met in the back right-hand corner of the church house. Pearl Sanders was interesting to listen to. She drew the boys into the lesson by asking questions. Otey was sitting on Tom's left. The boy to his right was less serious. Distracting Tom when Mrs. Sanders wasn't looking, the boy would bang his knee against Tom's knee and then mask his face with innocence. Tom had the urge to give him a good one. He couldn't find an opening to do it. The teacher seemed to be looking at him more than any of the rest of the class. Besides the Bible lesson in John's Gospel stimulated him. He ignored the pest and focused on Mrs. Sanders's words.

After Sunday School the young people went out to the front of the church for fresh air and idle talk. Tom found himself in a mixed circle. The pest was teasing the girls. The girls punctuated their whispers to one another with giggles. *Why,* thought Tom, *do girls always have to giggle?* Standing close to Otey, Tom excused himself and said he would see his friend at school. As he lumbered up the street toward home he was sure that he wasn't ready to start going to church. For the time being he thought Sunday School was enough.

On several occasions when Otey visited in the Maston home after football practice he and Nora teamed up to persuade Tom to become a Christian. In all honesty Tom responded, "I'm not sure whether I'm already a Christian or not." He continued, "It seems to me I'm livin' as good a life as the rest of you."

During his sophomore year in high school Tom made the football team as a substitute. He played every position at one time or another. It bothered him that he couldn't land a position on the first string. When he approached the coach about it, the retort came, "Tom, you're too good a substitute for me to sacrifice your help to the team by puttin' you in a fixed position." The next year he made first-string center. During his senior year the team elected him as their captain.

One weekend Central High played an away game in Asheville, North Carolina. In the first half of the game "Stinky" Davis suffered a severe kidney injury. Tom was playing at the time. He saw his friend in great pain lying on the field. The injured player was carried off on a stretcher and rushed to the hospital. After the game the team went to the train station for the return trip to Knoxville. Before departure word came from the hospital informing them that "Stinky's" condition was critical.

Soon the train pulled away from the Asheville station. It followed the French Broad River winding through the Smoky Mountains toward Tennessee. Inside the second-class coach the footballers were not their usual loud and boisterous selves. There were no rambunctious card games this time. Thoughts about the teammate they had left behind subdued them all. Tom agonized pondering about life itself. Why did this happen to "Stinky" and not to him? "Dear God, please don't let him die!" he pleaded silently. Then questions rushed over him: *What about me? . . . Am I ready to die? . . . I'm not sure, am I? . . . Should I have listened better to Otey and Nora?* Thoughts like these continued to torture him throughout the homeward journey. The overwhelming conclusion lept out at him that he was not ready!—that he really needed salvation!

The following week the Smithwood Baptist Church conducted its annual fall revival services. Tom was approaching his seventeenth birthday. On Monday evening at the supper table the conversation revolved around the meetings. Brother Wickham, the pastor of the church, was preaching. He was a big man—a native Texan. Tom knew him better as his high-school math teacher. Nora faced Tom across the table asking him to go to the service. Tom excused himself saying that he had too much homework. It was a pretext that covered up his intense struggle within. The elder Maston and Nora saw through it.

Every day that week walking to and from school Tom wrestled with himself spiritually. Remembering his friend "Stinky" Davis, he wondered how "Stinky" was doing in the hospital in far off Asheville. What if he died? Was "Stinky" ready? Was he—Tom Maston—ready? What is the meaning of life here and now? Is Tom in control? Who is in control? The questions were like a plague to him.

Every evening during the week, either Tom's father or

Nora invited Tom to the church meeting. Stubbornly, he refused by pleading his need to study. It was like the proverbial broken record. On Friday, Tom walked slowly home from football practice. With his cleats slung over his shoulder and his head hanging low, Tom approached the house. They had him backed into a corner. When the inevitable invitation came, Tom had no device to escape the revival. Homework on Friday night wouldn't do. With no football game that weekend, he was without any excuse. That's why, when his father asked him that evening, Tom capitulated. Reluctantly, he walked with them to the meeting.

Once inside the church house, Tom saw that it was full. The trio split. Samuel Maston went for his usual seat close to the pot-bellied stove on the right-hand side at the front. Nora spotted a friend who was saving a seat for her. Tom looked for Otey and didn't see him. He saw Winfred Marshall sitting toward the back. *What brings* him *to the revival?* he wondered. Winfred hadn't impressed him as being much of a Christian. Tom moved over to where his friend was sitting and squeezed in beside him.

In a low voice Winfred said, "Hey Tom, so you came too!"

Tom replied, "I couldn't get out of it. How 'bout you?"

"Nothin' better to do. So I came with my Mom," Winfred answered.

The meeting began with the hymn "There's a Land That Is Fairer than Day." The church house was alive with singing. Yet after the singing the service seemed to drag for Tom. One of the brothers read from the Bible.

There were others called on to lead in prayer. The prayers were long and fervent. Finally, Brother Wickham got up to preach. Tom thought the preacher should instead have a blackboard behind him and a piece of chalk in his hand. The boy couldn't think of him as anything other than his math teacher. The sermon was loud, but it didn't stir Tom. The truths issuing from the pulpit were only slightly more interesting than math problems.

As the cadence of the sermon diminished, there was movement in the back of the church. A small group of believers formed an informal circle of prayer. The sounds of praying pierced Tom's awareness. A spiritual dynamic was at work. Someone broke out singing, "Just as I am, without one plea," and the entire congregation joined in, "But that thy blood was shed for me,/And that thou bidd'st me come to thee,/O Lamb of God, I come! I come!" The singing shook Tom to his inner soul. He felt broken. Trembling, Tom dropped his head on the pew in front of him. He began to weep. Brother Wickam led into the gospel invitation for sinners to come to Jesus.

Winfred leaned forward and put his arm around Tom whispering his question, "What's wrong, Tom?"

In a plaintive voice, Tom squeezed out the words, "I wish I could accept the pastor's invitation."

Winfred assured him, "You can, if you will."

Immediately Tom sprung up from his seat, pushed out past the row of persons between him and the aisle, and bolted forward.

Years later Maston recollects the experience of moving

toward the pastor and at the same time glancing in the direction of his father. He recalls,

> Turning around I saw my old Daddy . . . He was doing something that I saw him do one other time and is the only person that I have ever seen doing that. He was laughing and weeping at the same time. Tears were streaming down his face but he was laughing.

Maston continues,

> If I interpret correctly what happened to me that night it was there back behind those pews . . . I said, 'I will,' and when one says, 'I will,' to God he surrenders his will to do the Lord's will.

On Sunday morning, two days later, Tom set out across the pasture toward the church house. Pausing at the gap in the fence a vivid thought "washed over him." He said to himself, "These two days with Jesus have been worth more than all the rest of my life!"

At the conclusion of a week of revival meetings neither the pastor nor the faithful were likely to have rated it a success. When Brother Wickham baptized Tom there was only one other, a grown man, to go into the water. There was the temptation to moan, "All that effort and only two additions to the church!" However, contrary to the human viewpoint, in the kingdom of God angels read statistics differently: "Likewise, I say unto you, there is joy in the presence of the angels of God over one sinner that repenteth" (Luke 15:10). In this case there were two. One of those became a mighty influence in the kingdom.

Calling

In the ensuing weeks Tom Maston exulted in the glow of joy. He had reached life on a higher plane. One Sunday between Sunday School and the morning worship he went with Otey to a nursery to get flowers to give to a sick friend in Sunday School. Arriving late during the service they slipped into the back of the church house. Brother Wickham was already into his sermon. Speaking in conversational mode he said one thing that jumped out at Tom. "I have been praying that the Lord would lay his hand on some of the young people of this church." It struck Tom in his inner core. The distinct feeling came over him that the preacher's words were intended mainly for his ears and heart. Instinctively he avoided greeting Brother Wickham at the door after the congregation was dismissed.

Several weeks later after the morning service, the pastor took Tom somewhat by surprise as they shook hands. "Mornin' Tom. Say, I've been meanin' to ask you this question: What course are you taking at school?"

"Manual arts, sir," the boy replied.

"Well," continued Brother Wickam, "If it means anything to you, I suggest that you think about taking the Latin course."

From that brief interchange at the entrance of the church on that Sunday, Maston understood that his pastor sensed that he, Tom Maston, had a call to preach. He, too, was beginning to wonder if it might be so. For weeks Tom grappled with one of life's bedrock decisions. The pastor's statement kept ringing in his awareness: "I suggest that you think about taking the Latin course." It triggered questions that obsessed Tom. He was haunted by: *What shall I study? What shall I become? What do I want to do with my life? What does God want of me? Am I Called To Preach?*

Finally he resolved that God indeed wanted him to become a preacher. In that time a young man with a divine call to Christian service had only two options. He could either be a preacher or a missionary. Tom definitely wasn't ready for the latter. He decided that it must be preaching. He walked with that decision for several days before he was willing to reveal it.

Again it was in a service at the Smithwood church that Tom took momentous action. With unflinching resolve he moved forward when the closing hymn began. It was almost a reenactment of the invitation service when he was converted. He glanced over at his father. Once more Samuel Maston was crying and laughing at the same time! When Tom reached the pastor, they joined hands. Tom simply said, "I feel that God has called me to preach."

Brother Wickham waited for the singing to stop. Then, he informed the congregation, "Tom Maston has something to share with you."

Tom was very nervous. In a low shaky voice he repeated what he had said to the pastor, "I feel that God has called me to preach," adding, "and I need your prayers."

After the benediction Tom was still standing at the front. Several of the older members came to him to shake his hand. One said, "Young man, I'm not surprised."

Another offered, "I have known this all along."

In the months that followed Tom experienced some uncertainty about the shape of his calling. The notion that his experience of calling was invalid never entered his mind. Instead, he struggled with the matter of how. "How will I serve the Lord?" he asked himself. Somehow he could not feel comfortable with the idea of being a pastor. Confusion arose because the first generation of the twentieth century didn't have a name for the kind of service God intended Tom Maston to perform. This was the major puzzle that Tom would agonize over for the next eight-to-ten years. Upon reflection much later in life, he realized that the call to preach was the only way God could get through to him: *God had to call me to preach if he called me at all. I knew no other call. He had to speak the language I could understand.* Step by step the puzzle would evolve into clearer resolution.

The following spring, father and son were working together in the fields. An oppressive sun ruled in the morning sky. Chopping corn is a wearisome task when it's solo work. Two can evade the drudgery of it by working the corn rows side by side. It lends itself to conversation and cheerful banter. This is especially true when the pair is as compatible as were Samuel Maston and his younger son. In the middle of a row, they stopped to rest. Leaning on the handle of his hoe Tom said, "You know, Dad, I feel called to preach. But for some reason that I cannot understand, I do not think that the Lord ever wants me to be a pastor of a church."

The elder Maston sighed. He drawled out his words, "My boy, as long as you feel that way about it, don't be ordained. There's too many ordained preachers in these hills that don't preach." Those words burned into young Tom's heart.

No doubt those very words gave him the resolve in later years to resist ordination to the gospel ministry. He was later ordained as a deacon in the Gambrell Street Baptist Church of Fort Worth, Texas. His refusal to be ordained to the ministry has certainly not been a deterrent to frequent forays into the pulpit. There have been many times when he has been a supply preacher. On one occasion he was interim pastor of a small congregation. Of course, popular demand has enlisted him as a speaker for youth meetings, denominational conferences, chaplains' retreats, mission meetings, and other such events throughout his long life. Indeed the opportunities have been superabundant.

The ensuing year after his graduation from Central High School Tom worked with his father on the farm. He had determined to enroll at Carson-Newman College in Jefferson City, Tennessee. Before he left the farm he wanted his labor to count the most for his hardworking Dad.

One day they were toiling in the back patch beyond the timber west of the house. They were digging potatoes—turning them up with a horse and plow. The time came for beast and farmhands to rest. They unhitched the mare and brought her into the shade of an oak tree at the edge of the field. The pair alternated swigs of water from a bottle. It was premeditated refreshment. Samuel Maston began speaking in serious tones:

My boy, I have something that I want to share with you before you go to college. I have known that the Lord was going to lay his hands on you or "Red", one or the other, since you were about four years of age. Some folks thought that I was called to preach. I struggled with it for some time and was uncertain.

He had, in fact, done some lay preaching when Tom was a young child. In the intervening years, however, he resisted all such activity. He had even refused to be ordained as a deacon in the church somehow expressing his feeling of unworthiness.

The father continued,

I told the Lord one time, "I am not sure You are calling me to preach; however, I do not see how I could support my growing family on what I can get from the churches that I could serve with the limited education that I have. Here are my two boys. I want You to take one of them in my place."

The words washed over Tom's heart. The father had reinforced his son with an unforgettable affirmation. Many times those indelible words have returned to assure the son in his adult career. Much later Maston recalls that "Red" often commented, "You are doing what Dad would have liked to have done if he had had the education to do it."

Reflecting on his father's memorable revelation, Maston suggested, "I have felt through the years that I needed to do a little extra for Dad and for Sis." Tom's sister had confided something to him later in life. She had experienced an early calling to Christian service and had rejected it. In addition to his father's mandate, Tom accepted the burden of his sister's failure in the pursuit of his own calling.

The puzzle of how God wanted Tom to fulfill his calling was still unclear. His first sermon was a disappointing experience. It provided him with an early clue. Brother Wickam had invited Tom to preach on the last Sunday before he went off to college. It was a banner day for the Maston family. Lucy Cooper, a youth worker from the Broadway Baptist Church of Knoxville, came to the service. She had befriended Tom earlier when they met at a Baptist youth event in Knoxville. Her help to the young preacher boy counted for much in his tender years.

The sermon was quite unmemorable. The elderly Maston cannot recall the text, the topic, or any of the content. It is probably the function of selective memory or, rather, selective forgetfulness. One reason the sermon is suspect relates to Lucy Cooper. After the service she greeted him. Her honest response to him came from a kind heart but it came forthrightly. She said, "Remember, Tom, the greatest sermon you'll ever preach is the life you live." This word certainly didn't encourage him about his sermon. But it did give him a bench mark on which to base his life.

Tom doesn't remember any comments that might have come from his father about the sermon. No doubt Samuel Maston was simply proud that his son had stood in the pulpit to declare divine truths. At least he dove off the diving board. So what if it was a belly flop? Tom's father was ever the encourager. He impacted the life of his son as the premier influence.

During the Great Depression when Maston was a professor doing graduate work at Yale University he wrote a tribute to his father. The letter is dated March 13, 1933, and was prompted by his father's surgery for a malignancy. Samuel Maston passed away that very month soon after Tom sent the letter. It is a masterpiece of filial devotion. Some excerpts serve to reveal something of this remarkable father-son relationship:

> A great deal of what I am now I know I owe to you. Your influence in my life has been greater than anyone who has touched it. I have said many times that you are the best man I have ever known. You have always been so sincere and genuine.

These two points: that his father was both the greatest influence and the "best man I have ever known" were affirmed by the aged Maston fifty-four years later as still true.

The letter continued with a focus on specifics:

> I have thanked the Lord many, many times that He gave me the opportunity of working with you those years on the farm. I learned more Bible and doctrines from you during those years than from any teacher I have had since in college or seminary. And what was more important I think I caught something of your spirit. I never can forget nor get away from the influence of those chats we used to have at the end of the corn rows, when we talked about

the most serious problems of the universe and the deepest possible religious problems.

Maston expressed his gratitude for the consistent encouragement his father always gave him on the long road of educational preparation. He cited an incident that still inspires him:

> One little thing that happened . . . has greatly influenced my life. I am sure you will not remember the incident. I had been down home from Carson-Newman for the weekend. I was leaving to go back to school. You were at the barn doing something. You stepped out to tell me goodbye. We stood and chatted a little while and as we shook hands you put your big left hand upon my shoulder and said, "My boy, do not let them take your power away from you." I did not know that I had any power, but the further I have gone in the educational process the more I have seen that there is a great deal of need for that warning of yours and the Lord has used that warning to help me retain, I hope, some of the spiritual warmth I had then.

He closed the letter with an affectionate outburst, ". . . you have been a mighty good Daddy to me . . . Wish I could sit down with you now for one of our chats." He would not see his father again in this life.

Missions

Samuel Maston's encouragement of his son persisted after Tom went off to college. Later during Tom's struggle over the direction of his call he considered missions. His father sanctioned the idea. Such encouragement was not the case with his mother. She always wanted her family to be near her. When Tom proposed to go to seminary in Texas, Sarah Maston strongly protested the thought of his separation for such a distance. Imagine how she must have felt about his going to Africa or China! Tom's father was the opposite. When the boy suggested the possibility of foreign missions the elder Maston simply said, "My boy, anything the Lord wants you to do is perfectly all right with me."

Tom's earlier rejection of the possibility of a call to missions changed to affirmation during his college career. It was part of the puzzle. Missions grew larger in his awareness through contact with furloughing missionaries on campus. In his private prayer life he would frequently promise the Lord that he would go anywhere and do anything that God willed. Customarily he would then crawl in bed tumbling and tossing uncomfortably. He knew within himself that he had not been honest in his prayer. God's Spirit was troubling his soul.

One night in his room in old Davis Hall once again he knelt by his bed and prayed the same words. Maston recollects vividly,

> . . . but that night I meant it. I remember going to the window and looking toward the Smoky mountains in the distance [in the moonlight]. And then there was a quiet peace in my heart because I knew that I was willing to go.

Tom eagerly sought other ways to continue his journey into servanthood. The missionary dimension was large for him. During his junior year W. D. Hudgins, Director of

Sunday School and the Baptist Young People's Union [BYPU] for Tennessee Baptists, spoke on campus. Hudgins' words motivated Tom to a high level of excitement. The speaker was enlisting workers for a summer missions program. In pairs they would itinerate in the rural areas of the state. One would instruct on methods for Sunday School work while the other would teach about the BYPU. It appealed to Tom as rural missions. He experienced a distinct desire to enlist and took an action that he had never before nor since taken: he *applied* for a position. He got the job.

The first summer he teamed with a student from The Southern Baptist Theological Seminary, David Livingstone. He was a mature young preacher who exerted a considerable influence on young Maston. He learned from his companion better ways of approaching and reaching persons for Christ. During that summer in rural Tennessee Tom began to understand himself better. His teammate demonstrated such excelling gifts for preaching and ministry that Tom became convinced that his gifts were in another direction. "I felt more at ease with a piece of chalk in my hand standing before a blackboard than I did standing behind the pulpit," he later recalled. Very slowly the picture was becoming clearer.

Tom began to seek out like-minded fellow students. On the campus of Carson-Newman College there was a Student Volunteer Band. It was a local affiliate of the interdenominational organization for mission volunteers which began in the latter part of the nineteenth century. The founding of the Student Volunteer Movement was inspired and encouraged by Dwight L. Moody. It had grown to become a truly international movement. In the first three decades of its existence it thrust forward some twenty-thousand Protestant missionaries around the world.

During his senior year, Tom was President of the Student Volunteer Band. At the same time he held the office of Vice president of the Student Volunteer Convention of Tennessee. He attended the annual national assembly of the organization in Des Moines, Iowa, farther from home than he had ever been. He was beginning to use his spiritual passport in his journey toward servanthood. The notable Christians that spoke at the meeting stirred the large gathering of students. They ignited Tom's enthusiasm. Robert E. Speer and John R. Mott fired his zeal for a world needing the Christian message.

It was the first time he had ever heard the superb Southern Baptist pulpiteer, George W. Truett. His message was particularly memorable. Maston still recalls the text that goes, "And David . . . served his day and generation" (Acts 13:36*a*). Maston also remembers the barest outline of the sermon: (1) And *David;* (2) And David *Served;* (3) And David Served *His Day and Generation.*

A remarkable coincidence occurred when former Congressman Walter H. Judd spoke in chapel at Southwestern Baptist Seminary. Maston was still active on the faculty. Judd had been a Methodist missionary to China before his service in the United States Congress. In his chapel message, Judd referred to the same Student Volunteer Convention in Des Moines. He mentioned that it was his first time to hear Truett. Then he proceeded to give the *same sermon outline*! At the end of the chapel service, Maston rushed to the platform to meet Judd and to introduce himself. They spent some delightful moments comparing notes about the Des Moines meeting. It must have been a watershed occasion. Maston's own son Gene relates reading in a book by Elton Trueblood that he had attended the very same Student Volunteer Convention.

Essie Mae

Carson-Newman College not only equipped Tom with a good education drawing him toward missions but also gave him a lifelong companion. Essie Mae McDonald chose Carson-Newman, turning down a full scholarship at the University of Chattanooga. She was consistently an outstanding student through high school, college, and seminary. Tom Maston soon recognized that she was the kind of life companion he needed. She descended from a Southern Appalachian ancestry that issued from that corner of Tennessee and Georgia where the Battle of Chickamauga had been fought.

The two got acquainted as leaders in organizations on campus and at church. In the Student Volunteer Band Tom was president and Essie Mae secretary. In the Baptist Young People's Union at the First Baptist Church of Jefferson City they reversed roles. She was president and he was the secretary. During their college days they did not date much if at all. Campus rules and heavy study schedules disallowed frequent dating. However, "Where there's a will there's a way." It became necessary to have frequent officers' meetings of the two organizations! No dates—only officers' meetings!

Eventually in their junior year they became serious. Tom was acutely aware that Essie Mae was the *one* for him. On May 18, a warm Sunday in 1919, they prearranged a date. The only time allowed for dating was Sunday afternoon. After lunch in the dining hall, Tom went to his room in Davis Hall to prepare for this crucial turning point in his life. He knew that he was going to pop the question. Kneeling in the customary spot beside his bed, Tom prayed for divine guidance.

At that very moment in the Sarah Swan Home across the campus, Essie Mae was kneeling beside her bed. She had known that Tom loved her very much. It was mutual love. She prayed fervently for God's wisdom. With an assured heart she started out for their tryst.

Armed with similar confidence, Tom cantered across campus to their rendezvous. He breathed deeply of the sweet fragrance of flowering trees. The campus was alive with the brilliance of an East Tennessee springtime. He waited for her at the side entrance of the recently built administration building. In a minute he saw her walking briskly toward him. His heart quickened. They greeted without physical contact. Holding hands was a campus taboo.

Nearby, there was a sled abandoned at the top of a slope. It had been orphaned by a careless sledder months before in snow time. The couple sat on it and began talking. Tom started by reading a stanza from a poem he had written for her:

Will you be a partner with me?
Will you go with me through life;
Share with me its joy and strife—
Working for God far over the sea?
Now to this what do you say
My own, my dearest Essie Mae?

He paused and enquired, "What would you think about our planning to spend our lives together?" There was anxious silence for the briefest eternity.

She responded in a deliberate manner, "Yes, I'd like that." Tom's heart soared.

He jubilantly shared with her his experience of praying in his room before the date. When she confided that she, too, had prayed, he was overwhelmed. Later in life he recalled, "Well you can understand after all that how neither the devil nor high water could've ever kept us apart!"

After sixty-five years of marriage she reflects on his earlier bent for poetry. Often, she says, he would write poems during their long separation in the summer months. That was before they wed. "After their marriage —no more poetry," she said laughingly.

They kept their engagement a secret for the most part of the next two years until shortly before the wedding. It was mostly Essie Mae's desire. Her favorite flower is the daisy because "daisies don't tell." She didn't want it to be spread around like so much campus gossip. The thought of friends and fellow students teasing her about Tom was too much to bear. Their relationship was too sacred to be cheapened by such prattle. On the other hand, it amused her immensely when some of her friends would say, "Essie Mae, you goin' ta let Tom Maston get away?"

The bond that love forged between Tom and Essie Mae enhanced the mission awareness of both together. She later recalled, "All the time we were in college . . . our goal in life [was] going to the mission field."

Maston offered, "In college, we'd thought more about Africa than anywhere else because the only missionary that we could remember coming to our college campus was a missionary from Africa." "Miss Olive" they had called her. Olive Edens, a graduate of Carson-Newman, resided during her first furlough on the campus. She was a Southern Baptist missionary to Nigeria. It was their senior year.

A year after their engagement in the spring of 1920, Tom and Essie Mae faced a momentous decision. They determined that they would go to seminary the following fall after their graduation from college. Further they determined that they would attend the same institution together as singles for at least a year before getting married. The decision lay between two seminaries. Essie Mae had already been offered a full scholarship at the Woman's Missionary Training School at Southern Baptist Theological Seminary, Louisville, Kentucky. That was very tempting. Tom's interest lay in the direction of a fairly new school, Southwestern Baptist Theological Seminary in Fort Worth, Texas. Neither would insist on one of the two choices.

With the matter still undecided at the beginning of the

summer Tom went off to the summer missions program. They set a bold plan. Separated by distance they would ponder and pray about the decision. On a given date each would write to the other his or her personal choice. The letters were mailed so that they would cross en route. When the letters were received and opened it was unanimous that they would go to Southwestern!

For part of the summer he teamed with Ullin Leavell in the mountain communities of East Tennessee. Ullin interupted his summer work briefly to go to Richmond for missionary appointment to China by the Foreign Mission Board of the Southern Baptist Convention. Tom was thrilled to be working with a bona fide missionary.

Taken part of the way to their first assignment, they were deposited at a prearranged place. At that point they were to meet a second driver who would deliver them to the destination. They found themselves standing on the side of a wide shallow stream where the road ran through the water. The bank was lined with a margin of flat smooth rocks.

After five or ten minutes the temptation grew too strong. "Come on, Ullin," said Tom, "let's go skip some rocks while we wait for our ride."

The two started picking up rocks and began a contest to see which one could make the longest string of skips. A car or two splashed through the ford but didn't stop to offer a ride. The pair continued their sport for well over an hour. Finally they decided their ride wasn't coming at all. They flagged a car and begged a farmer to take them to the appointed community. Fortunately he was going in that direction. When they arrived late in the day their hosts asked them why they failed to show up at the prearranged location. Carefully they described the place where they had waited. A man spoke up, "Waal, I went a lookin' fer y'all at the ford. I didn't see nobody looked like they's comin' for this kinda' work. All I seen was two *kids* skippin' rocks."

The faces of Tom and Ullin turned red. With considerable embarrassment they owned up to it. "Why that was us," said Ullin. "We're sorry we didn't look up to see you when you came by," he offered. At that point Tom considered that the week ahead was going to be more of an education for him and Ullin than for the mountain folk.

If one is willing to learn, the people of the Southern Appalachians can enhance one's knowledge substantially. Tom began to recognize that the passive activities of observing, listening, and learning are a crucial part of any kind of missionary endeavor. Adjusting to the culture opened doors.

Tom and Ullin spent one week in a community in Sevier County with a house that had screens. The house belonged to the local squire. The young men were thrilled at the idea of staying in a home that would be relatively free of flies. That was a banner week.

A mountain woman from back in one of the coves came to the course every day. From the first day she invited the young teachers to go home with her at noon to eat. In the middle of the week after postponing it for one reason or another Tom told Ullin that he thought they should go. Ullin declined saying that he wasn't feeling well. He thought it best that he remain in the house that had screens. Tom determined to go even if he had to go alone.

At the end of the morning session, Tom struck out on foot with the woman up a mountain road. They wound through the hills and turned up into a cove. The weather was hot and humid, and he was glad when they reached the small frame house. It sported a coat of white paint from the previous spring. As they entered the gate in the front fence he observed a neat and tidy yard. Inside the house the floors were swept clean and the furniture had obviously been dusted. Of course, there were no screens.

He shook hands with the woman's husband. The big calloused hands reminded Tom of his daddy. The woman then introduced her unmarried adult daughter who lived with them. The man offered him a chair at the fireplace end of the big room. There was no need for a fire. Tom asked the man about his crops. The man expressed surprise and pleasure that the young man could talk sensibly about things that mattered most to him—what to feed hogs, how to dig potatoes, and such. They talked a long time while the two women put the meal on the table.

When the woman finally called them to the kitchen end of the room to eat, Tom had a man-sized appetite working inside him. The table challenged his hunger. It was covered with mouth-watering food. There was sausage that had been canned from the previous fall's hog killing and a plate piled high with pan-fried potatoes. The daughter brought a plate of hot cornbread and set it on the table next to a big pitcher of fresh milk. On the work table next to the stove he spied a freshly baked apple pie. It was a Smoky Mountain feast!

Tom had been so busy focusing on the food that he had barely noticed the strange contraption that hung over the table. Suspended from the ceiling was an old-style fly whisk, a homemade brush-like device rigged with string and a pulley. The cord was strung so that it dropped down to the floor at one end of the table. It was at the end where the mountaineer sat. The cord was attached to a foot pedal. The man controlled the motion of the fly whisk, moving it slowly back and forth the length of the table.

There were no flies on the food at the table! Tom glanced over at the apple pie. It relieved him to see that it had been covered with a cloth. He thought about other occasions when in a mountain cabin the flies were so thick that with a raisin pie one couldn't tell the pie from the flies!

The square meal was over more quickly than it took to prepare. Tom had acquitted himself well. Politely he excused himself explaining that he had a meeting with some young people at the church and needed to prepare for it. He could hardly wait to get back to Ullin to tell him what he missed. He was going to rub it in big. Down the mountain road he hastened.

Reaching the squire's house he bounded up the steps and entered the house. Tom rushed into the room and found Ullin stretched out on the bed reading a book. "Ullin," he began, "that was the best meal that I've had. The place was so clean. Even the front yard was swept. And the daughter's bare feet were as clean as could be. And there were no flies at the table! You really missed it."

He then proceeded to describe the mountaineer's fly-whisk contraption.

When he started to describe the tasty food, Ullin interrupted in disbelief, "Aw come on, Tom, you're just joshin' me."

The summer sped by rapidly. It had been a growing experience. Even though he was going to Texas for his seminary education, he determined to return to Tennessee again the next summer. For five summers in a row he worked in the program. After their wedding Essie Mae joined him for the last three years. It truly was a proving ground for his talents. In his later years Maston considers that, ". . . this definitely contributed something to my interest in missions and also quite a little bit to my teaching methods . . ."

In the fall of 1920 Tom and Essie Mae traveled to Fort Worth, Texas, to launch their long tenure on Seminary Hill. They both enrolled in the religious education school of Southwestern Baptist Theological Seminary. It was a three-year course. Though it was not a requirement, they both took Greek. Essie Mae made as good grades as did Tom.

Part of the spiritual baggage which they brought to the seminary was a zeal for missions. Tom worked on campus as a waiter in the dining hall. He was assigned to wait on the table of the W. B. Bagbys, Southern Baptists' first missionaries to Brazil. This afforded him the exciting chance to get closely acquainted with some missionary veterans. They impressed him as very approachable.

However, early in their seminary experience, Tom

began to entertain doubts about whether their calling was to a foreign destination. Essie Mae confessed that she was also struggling with it. Toward the end of the first academic year they sought counsel from the professor of Missions, W. H. Knight. His questioning probed about how much longer they expected to be in seminary. When they replied that it would take two more years, he suggested patience. "You have plenty of time to work through it," he said.

With one year of seminary behind, Tom and Essie Mae looked forward to an eventful summer. They planned to marry in June. First they returned to Tennessee to work in the summer missions effort. They were paired separately in the early part. A one-week break was all they could afford for the wedding. The ceremony was at her parents' home near Chattanooga. Floral decorations made of daisies brightened the room. Remember? "Daisies don't tell." The bride and groom returned to their engagement in rural missions. They acquiesced to a working honeymoon in the Tennessee mountains for the rest of the summer.

In one of the communities where Tom and Essie Mae worked, a family by the name of Rule furnished the newly-weds accommodation. It was a small house. Under the circumstances, it was kept fairly clean. With no screens, there certainly were flies. Best of all, the chickens had free run of the kitchen! Five or six children made it a full house. Some of the finest Baptist leaders in Tennessee came out of that family.

The whole family went to church for the training course. The first evening when they marched back to the house, they all stopped on the porch and sat down. Mr.

Rule said, "Now somebody bring the lamp and the Book."
An older child dutifully went inside the house to fetch the
lamp and the family Bible. The father read a Scripture
portion leaning forward in his chair to catch the lamp-
light. One of the older children led in prayer. Then immediately the whole family group burst forth in song. Lustily
they sang the old hymns of faith. The sound of their
singing reverberated through the hills and coves. For the
newlyweds it was an unforgettable experience.

The children all went to bed. The young couple visited
for a while with Mr. and Mrs. Rule. At bedtime the
woman showed them their room. They slept soundly except that very early in the morning they were awakened
by the sound of many feet tramping through the room.
Later they learned that all the children slept in a lean-to
attached as an extension to their bedroom. The only access
was through their room!

Here in the mountains there was a somewhat different
culture than what either of them had known. A week with
someone like the Rule family enlightened and inspired the
young couple. The marriage was having its baptism in
missionary service. It was rural missions.

Returning to the Texas seminary in the fall, they realized that the puzzle of their missionary calling was still
unsolved. There was a visiting professor of missions—
Robert T. Bryan, a thirty-six-year veteran of missions in
China on furlough. It was the last furlough for him and
Mrs. Bryan before retiring. Coming under the influence of
this gray-headed, bespectacled gentleman renewed the
missionary vision for Tom and Essie Mae.

The leading question that might have provided the clue to their calling concerned geography. There was never a doubt that the Lord wanted them in his service. The nagging question was where? In college it was Africa—thanks to Miss Olive Edens. During their first year in seminary it was South America. The Bagbys were partly responsible for that leaning. Their friendship with Anne Laseter, a fellow student heading for Chile, reinforced their Latin American connection. Now the latest was China. At that time, over half of all Southern Baptist missionaries served in China. Therefore, they had several friends who either had already gone to China or were preparing to go there. Ullin Leavell and his new bride had just recently sailed for China. Then there was Dr. Bryan right there on campus motivating an immediate interest in China.

The couple would sometimes go for a walk in the late evening to discuss their quandary. Once they strolled southward from campus on Crowley Road in the direction of an old schoolhouse. Hand-in-hand they thrashed over their options.

"I'm impressed with the opportunities for educational missionaries in Chile," mused Tom aloud. "Anne says that the work is new, and it's a small mission. I'd like that."

"True enough," chimed in Essie Mae. "But even though the work in China is much older and has a larger group of missionaries, don't forget that it is a much larger country. It's just chock full of people. Compared to the population, the missionaries are really very few. And the school work is growing. It's such a challenge."

After a thoughtful pause and a few more steps southward, Tom said, "The truth of the business is that I wish
we were two couples instead of one. Then one could go to
China and the other to Chile."

"Oh, Tom," Essie Mae replied, "I know what you mean
but that doesn't really solve anything."

"I know," he sighed. "Somehow we've just got to resolve this. It's so hard not knowing where the Lord wants
us." They turned to amble homeward.

During their second year in the seminary, they both
developed their scholarly competence. Summer saw them
back in Tennessee doing rural missions. This dual emphasis on scholarship and practical application became a Maston hallmark.

At the beginning of Tom's third year J. M. Price, head
of the school of religious education, invited Tom to substitute in the classroom for him. Price absented himself from
the campus for special studies during the first semester.
For Tom it was a baptism of teaching. Still he continued
with his own studies.

At the same time the gentle but persistent influence of
Bryan grew in their awareness. More and more China
tugged at their hearts. They became increasingly convinced that China was to be their place of service. They
realized that the Bryans were expecting to conclude their
furlough and return to China at the end of the fall semester in the beginning of 1923. Without applying pressure
Dr. Bryan had, nevertheless, induced them to consider
traveling back to China with him.

An obstacle confronted Tom and Essie Mae. The Bryans were scheduled to depart in the middle of the academic year at the beginning of Tom and Essie Mae's last semester at Southwestern. Going to China seemed to be so closely wrapped up with traveling together with the Bryans. They attempted to accelerate their degree program by taking a required correspondence course in church history. The tactic failed. The Bryans departed without them. China was put on the shelf.

Dr. Price returned to the campus and to the classroom for the second semester of the 1922-23 academic year. Tom had assumed that he would concentrate only on his studies to complete his degree program. Price had something else in mind. To Tom's surprise Price asked him again to continue his student teaching. He taught two more courses that semester.

Tom was beginning to understand that his calling was definitely as a teacher. It could either happen in some foreign land or right here in his homeland. It might be somewhere among the churches. His experiences in summer missions and now at the Seminary encouraged him to see this more clearly. The puzzle fell more into place. It might well not be foreign missions. What a revolutionary thought! Essie Mae was not so ready to accept this. It made their frequent walks very stimulating.

Graduation in the spring featured Tom as class speaker —a graduate from the school of religious education? What a remarkable precedent! At the conclusion of the ceremony faculty and students were herded to the front of Fort Worth Hall for the taking of the class picture. While Tom and Essie Mae were walking toward the front steps L. R.

Scarborough, the seminary president, came alongside. He slipped his arm under Tom's and pulling him to one side said in a firm voice, "Tom, it looks like we may need you here."

It was a thunderclap from the blue sky. It struck at the decisive crossroads of their servanthood. The key piece fell into place in their puzzle. China was pushed onto the shelf. Foreign missions began to fade as an option. A new visa was stamped in his passport. It was the visa for a lifelong journey into servanthood as an extraordinary teacher.

2
Miles to Go

T. B. Maston, servant-pilgrim, embarked on a variegated career. It developed into a kaleidoscope of roles. Look through the eyepiece, reader; twist the tube: teacher—stalwart—teacher—student—teacher—missions advocate—teacher—counselor—teacher—Mission Board confidant—teacher—trusted colleague—teacher—author—teacher—denominational reformer—teacher—champion of ethics—teacher—missions traveler—teacher. Always Maston is *teacher.*

Professor Maston

Maston plunged into teaching as a third-year student at Southwestern Seminary in 1922. From the start he taught ethics. It marked the beginning of a forty-one-year teaching ministry at that institution. "I'd rather teach than eat," Maston said at his retirement. "I've never taught a class that I didn't enjoy," he insisted.

He ranks among the elite few who have taught in the faculties of religious education and theology. In 1937 he was listed as teaching in both schools. He offered virtually every course in the religious education curriculum. In addition to ethics, Maston's specialties were social work, student work, youth work, and church recreation. He pioneered offering a course on recreation in a theological institution. The first published work by Maston was on recreational leadership in the churches.

Maston's vocation in teaching did not diminish missionary his fervor, however. Befriended missionaries corresponded with the Mastons from the far fields where Southern Baptists were serving. Maston had a knack for rapport with missionaries and for understanding their problems. A flow of letters from friends maintained their warm feeling, especially for China.

In the spring of 1931 the Mastons received a letter from China. Blanche Groves, an educational missionary assigned to Yates Academy in Soochow wrote it during a journey to Nanking. She penned an eight-page epistle in installments en route. The circumstances were exceptional: ". . . some of it written on a rocking train, some on a motor launch, some sitting on my suitcase at a station." She poured out her heart describing "the *most serious* situation I've faced in China." It was a crisis threatening the very existence of mission schools. "Dr. Maston," she wrote, "I would give worlds if I could talk with you this afternoon. Somehow, you seemed to understand mission problems so clearly. And you could pray intelligently about our situation."

The letter arrived during the peak of the so-called "Great Depression." The fledgling seminary in Texas was going through a crisis of its own. It summoned the faculty at Southwestern to great heights of loyalty. Virtually unbearable debt forced the Seminary to slash salaries in half.

Even so it could actually only pay what was received in the treasury. Sometimes it was half-of-the-half or even less. Therefore, the professors endured at quarter salary or less. The administration had to ask only a few to resign. However, some felt compelled to leave for better-supporting opportunities of service. The stouteheartedness of the professors who remained demonstrated a kind of missionary determination. Maston was among the tenacious ones.

A colleague with seniority in the school of religious education pleaded with Maston to resign. At the time Maston was the youngest member of the faculty. Maston discussed the matter with Dr. Price and Dr. Scarborough. They resisted the idea strongly, convincing the young professor to remain. The administrators insisted that instead the senior colleague was a poor teacher anyway and "He's got to go." It saddened Maston when eventually the man left because Maston considered him "one of the best men that ever lived."

During an excursion in his servant-journey Maston endured yet another crisis. In the fall of 1932 he piled his family—a wife and two little boys—into their car. Pulling a mounded two-wheel trailer they struck out for New Haven, Connecticut. Colleagues questioned the good sense of the ethics professor. Nevertheless, he enrolled in a doctoral program at Yale University.

Two weeks into the spring semester, 1933, while on the Yale campus one morning he fell acutely ill with a temperature of 104 degrees. The doctors gave the diagnosis— pneumonia! They could not offer an optimistic prognosis. He was kept in an oxygen tent for five days and in intensive care for two weeks. It was a close encounter with death.

At one time in a semi-conscious state he sensed that he was lying flat on his back on top of a narrow rail fence. He felt that if he extended his arm on either side the loss of balance would make him fall off the fence. In that precarious situation he experienced deep communion with God. He expressed his willingness to die if that was what God wanted. However, he pleaded that the Lord would spare him. There were two urgent reasons: "First, because of my two boys. I asked the Lord to let me live so they would grow up with a father. And, second, I did not feel that my work was done."

There was round-the-clock prayer for him on one occasion at their home church, the Gambrell Street Baptist Church in Fort Worth. After four weeks in the hospital he recuperated well enough to be released. Slowly through the spring and summer he regained health and strength. After their return to Seminary Hill one day he met professor Jeff Ray on campus. The venerable gentleman stopped, paused, and looked the younger man over top to bottom. "Tom," he said cautiously, "if it did not sound sacrilegious I would say that we wasted a lot of praying on you."

The illness delayed Maston's graduate studies. However, he persisted tenaciously and was awarded the PhD degree in 1939. During Maston's first semester after his return from Yale a seemingly harmless event occurred fifteen-hundred miles away. It reached out to impact his missionary heart considerably. The Foreign Mission Board in Richmond, Virginia, in its fall meeting of 1933 created a department of education and promotion. This was an early agenda of Charles E. Maddry in his first year as executive secretary of the board. The action triggered a search for a secretary to head the department.

Later Maddry visited Southwestern and spoke in chapel in Cowden Hall. In his introductory remarks he mentioned that the Foreign Mission Board was actively seeking someone for the position of secretary of education and promotion. The words stimulated resonant vibrations in Maston's heart. The opportunity gripped him firmly. The remainder of Maddry's message flew over Maston's head as he pondered the potential of the position.

The ensuing days dragged into weeks as the thought obsessed him. Maston grew convinced that he was the man for the new position at the Foreign Mission Board. The conviction was clear though modest. Given his persistent zeal for missions and his experience in education, Maston sensed that he had the qualifications for it. It would enable him to do a lot of writing. This reinforced an already-strong appeal. The idea preoccupied his days and nights. It was hard to fulfill the routine regimen of the classroom and other seminary responsibilities. It was even harder to sleep at night. The excitement of the new opportunity made him toss and turn in his bed for nights on end.

Maston was certain that the Lord was in it. However, he did not feel free to discuss it with any of his colleagues. He did confide, nevertheless, with his long-standing friend, Jerry Lambdin. Their friendship stemmed from earlier collaboration in Knoxville, Tennessee, in the Baptist Young People's Union organization at the associational level. At the time, Lambdin was Training Union secretary of the Sunday School Board. In that capacity, he had occasion to visit the Southwestern campus. On one such visit, Maston expressed his strong sense of leadership for the Foreign Mission Board position with his friend.

Lambdin suggested that his friend should let Maddry know of his interest. "Oh no," said Maston, "Jerry, you know me better than to suggest that. I could never be so bold in pushing myself. I simply mention it to you in case you have the opportunity and the inclination to suggest my name to Maddry." His friend consented.

Later, Lambdin was able to communicate Maston's interest in the new position to Maddry. For whatever reason, Maddry did not pursue the matter. Maston received no offer. There wasn't even an overture. In 1936, another man was elected to the Foreign Mission Board position. However, Maston remained solidly convinced at the time that the impression he had gained in chapel that day was of the Lord. His unwavering conviction about this has persisted throughout his long life and influenced his theology of the will of God.

Maston's popularity grew on campus. It increased steadily throughout his teaching career. He gained the reputation of one who manifested great empathy with his students. His lectures did not seem like lectures. A friendly conversational style opened up the students to the vision behind his teaching. He was the one faculty member who would play softball with the students. During the annual "faculty takeoff," the students gave a public roasting of their professors. Always they would find some student with glasses and a thick crop of hair to do an impersonation of Maston. It was hilarious as the student mimicked Maston's mannerisms complete with the wink of his eye. He would spout out characteristic phrases such as: "The truth of the business is . . ." When the students poked fun at Maston, he would always laugh heartily thoroughly enjoying their pleasure at his expense.

During his student days Keith Parks, current president of the Foreign Mission Board, recalls that often they would refer to Maston affectionately as "Uncle Tom." It was done in deep respect toward one who was a favorite.

Once when Parks was leaving the campus post office, he turned the corner and was suddenly face-to-face with Maston. Before he realized what he was saying Keith blurted out, "Hello, Uncle Tom." As soon as the irretrievable words left his lips the faint color of rose flooded his face.

With a broad smile on his face and a chuckle in his voice Maston replied, "Hello, Keith." Sheepishly, the student hastened his steps to avoid prolonging his embarrassment in conversation.

Parks affirms Maston as one of his favorite professors. "The authenticity of how his teachings and life matched up caused me to hold him in very high esteem . . . he really impacted my life more than anyone else."

Among the myriad of missionaries with whom Maston corresponded was the same Keith Parks. He remembers a question that arose in a classroom discussion in the Indonesian seminary during his first term of service. In their study of Acts chapter 15, some Indonesian students raised a question about the eating of congealed blood, a practice of the Chinese population in Indonesia. Parks wrote, "Dr. Maston, you taught us a lot of ethics but there are a few things you didn't cover. I want to know about this." He proceeded to give the students' question and the background of it. Maston replied clearly setting forth the modern-day application of ancient scriptural truths. Parks continued, "He was one of the few professors that I would write when I encountered something on the field . . . I felt like he would have some answers when I wrote him." Maston *never* failed to answer his correspondence.

Not all of the questions pertained to hypothetical classroom matters. Often missionaries would write for personal counsel. One letter came from a single missionary in South America. It began, "We value your opinion highly because of what you are and because of what your friendship means to us." She confided in Maston as the only person outside of family members. The young woman earnestly sought his "frank and honest opinion" about a marriage proposal from a Latin who was a respected Baptist leader. Her high regard and obvious affection for him were clearly expressed. There were problems, of course.

The reply is vintage Maston. He began, "In the final analysis the decision must be entirely yours." He then acknowledged that she seemed to understand the potential problems. He offered his own slant on the problem inviting her to think through some things she may have overlooked. In concluding he assured her with the urgent promise, "I shall be praying for you that you will do the thing that is right and the thing that is best for you, for all concerned, and most of all—for the cause of Christ."

The primary meaning of *master* is teacher. Maston exemplifies the meaning. He labored as a skilled workman in the craft of teaching. In the mid-1940s after the Second World War, Maston introduced a course on Christians facing the postwar world. He invited Frank Means, the professor of missions, to team-teach the course with him. Means would frequently stop to visit Maston in his office:

> He never seemed hurried or resentful because what he was doing had been interrupted. Dr. Maston was always prepared for class, . . . he was always hard at work—polishing notes, digesting reading, or writing.

Means described his approach to course preparation,

> Even then he followed the kind of schedule he follows today. He turns first to some Scripture passage for inspiration and instruction. Then he gives his attention to the project which has top priority at the moment. Less urgent matters come later.

Later when Means left the faculty to join the staff of the Foreign Mission Board, their friendship continued at a high level of mutual respect and confidence.

One measure of Maston's excellence as a teacher is that he demanded hard work of his students. William Estep, distinguished professor of church history at Southwestern, says of Maston, "I found no teacher who challenged me more to give my best to the study at hand . . . The rapport which he had with his students was truly remarkable."

Frequently Maston would reach the classroom just before the ringing of the bell. The students had cleared the corridor as he approached the door alone. He would pause for a moment and bow his head leaning forward so that his forehead softly touched the door. In that instant he would breath the prayer, "Oh Lord, help me to lead these students." He insists that on such an occasion, " . . . anything good that would happen was because the Holy Spirit was there with us."

Keith Parks says of Maston's teaching, ". . . he had as deep a commitment to missions as any professor that I had."

Another longtime friend on the Foreign Mission Board's staff, Charles Bryan, emphasizes, "He taught missions even though his subject matter was ethics."

Maston was my teacher. I remember well his course on "The Rural Church." Maston equipped students with some universal principles that apply well to the missionary situation. He stressed the need for sacrificial ministry to rural people. His emphasis on cultivating rural churches that grow in stewardship to stand firmly on their own resources likewise speaks to the missionary's situation. The professor's experiences in summer mission work in rural Tennessee served him well for illustrations in the course.

Maston played an unofficial role in missions in his capacity as professor. He became the confidant of many students who sought his wisdom. Many who came were mission volunteers. Some were seeking clarification of God's direction in their calling. His perceptive counsels reinforced them in crucial decision making. The problems and situations that students brought to him represented the spectrum of human experience. He was sometimes like a beacon pointing them away from dangerous waters.

This role made Maston a natural resource person for personnel consultants of the Foreign Mission Board who visited the Southwestern campus. The first to lean on him for assistance was Edna Frances Dawkins. Her visits extended regularly over a thirteen-year period. Often the two would confer, discussing particular students who were active candidates for missionary service. Maston felt more free to share his opinions in candor orally than in writing. Ms. Dawkins remembered that he was "always kind, but quite honest in his appraisal of a candidate." She recalled that his help went even further,

> This busy professor would take time almost every day to come by for a brief visit with me, to offer a word of encouragement, to ask if there was anyway that he might be of help to me, and to discuss candidates with me. His expression of confidence in me has played a vital part in my belief in myself and in God's ability to use me in . . . the foreign mission enterprise of Southern Baptists.

Dawkins consulted more with Maston than any other member of the faculty because she found him to be entirely fair and unbiased in his appraisals. Jesse Fletcher followed her as associate personnel secretary for the western United States. He also consulted freely with Maston. However, while Fletcher valued the professor's input, he found him to be a "biased informant" when the candidate in question was one of Maston's "boys." By this time, there was a significant increase in the number of students majoring in ethics.

There is no doubt about Maston's strong loyalty toward those who took their major with him. He exerted an immense influence toward missions among graduate students in the ethics Department. Maston interceded for Cecil Thompson upon the latter's completion of a Th.D. in ethics. Thompson and his wife sensed a calling to theological teaching in an overseas seminary. Since his major was ethics, and there were no requests for professors in that field, he wondered where the Lord would use him. Maston interceded. Shortly before their appointment as missionaries, Maston persuaded the administration of the Baptist Seminary in Buenos Aires, Argentina, to establish a Department of ethics. The Thompsons were subsequently appointed to the Argentine seminary. They served there for twenty years before transferring to the Spanish Baptist Publishing House in El Paso, Texas.

Ebbie Smith, professor of ethics and missions at Southwestern, went to Richmond years ago for missionary appointment. Someone at the Foreign Mission Board exclaimed with exasperation, "Another Christian ethics major! Why can't we get more theology people?"

In 1979 James Dunn, executive director of the Baptist Joint Committee on Public Affairs, wrote that among the forty-nine Th.D. graduates from Southwestern who majored in ethics, thirteen were actively serving as missionaries. The published statement that the total of doctoral-graduate missionaries who majored under Maston exceeds the number of missionaries representing any other department of any other Southern Baptist seminary is true.

A different twist in this pattern occurred in the case of Rodney Wolfard. In the mid-fifties, Maston was searching for a faculty addition to his department. Wolfard had the qualities and experience that Maston was looking for. He seriously considered inviting the younger man to take the position. However, he resisted doing so because Wolfard had just been appointed as a missionary to Brazil. Maston could not bear the thought of removing such a good man from missionary service.

By the time of his retirement, it is estimated that Maston had taught between eight and ten thousand students. Soon after Maston retired in 1963, he participated in a conference of missionaries in Salvador, Brazil. It is not surprising that thirty of the fifty-five missionaries attending were his former students.

Maston's role in guiding and boosting new missionaries extended beyond them to missionary veterans. He accepted the task of conserving those who were experiencing "burnout." Missionary James Musgrave illustrates Maston's compassionate help for wounded missionaries. He wrote,

> In 1952, I returned to the States with a broken body, a precarious hold on my emotions, fear that I might be mentally unsound, and with serious doubts about my ability to discern the will of God for my life. Things had gone so badly that I couldn't believe the events, in any way, tied

in with what experiencing God's will could mean. Dr. Maston shepherded me through this crisis while I struggled with acceptance of psychiatric treatment, checked out my inclination toward a medical education, and "waited on the Lord." My subsequent ability to walk the tightrope is due, in large part, to principles which Dr. Maston helped me to apply to my life. In other words, I don't think I would be on the mission field, and perhaps not even in the ministry, except for his help.

Gerald Riddell, missionary to Chile, relates his personal story of salvage. He engaged in graduate studies during a furlough from Columbia. His study carrel was next to the room Maston used for writing. The two had lengthy fruitful conversations. Riddell had come home much disillusioned about missionary service. The combination of ruptured relationships among missionaries and alienation between missionaries and nationals weighed heavily on him. In addition, there was strong Roman Catholic opposition.

All of this had taken its toll on the thirteen-year veteran. One afternoon he asked the professor for permission to absent himself from a seminar session. He explained that he had an appointment with a psychiatrist. Maston granted the request saying, "You're not the one that needs his head examined!" The gentle perceptive encouragement of the professor guided the missionary through his problems. When the Riddells were reassigned to Chile, Maston affirmed the decision. It proved to be a redemptive solution for all concerned.

The chapel service on Mission Day at Southwestern

Seminary over the years has been a watershed for missions. Maston has never been the speaker. On occasion, he has appeared on the platform to offer the prayer. More often than that he has stood at the front at the end of one of the four aisles to receive students coming forward during decision time.

On one such occasion, the students packed the auditorium. At the close of the message there was a call for commitment to missions. The singing had started as Maston and three other colleagues took their forward places facing the student congregation. He looked longingly at the faces before him. Most had solemn expressions as they sang. Others had heads bowed in prayer.

One face showed agony. As the young man tried to sing he could only manage the words haltingly. Maston recognized him immediately as Francis DuBose, one of his students. The professor remembered exactly where DuBose sat in class. Now he saw him steeped in spiritual agitation. Maston bowed his head earnestly praying. He asked the Lord to help his student resolve his muddled soul and come to a clear decision. Immediately, DuBose pushed out of his place toward the aisle and moved forward to reach for the outstretched hand of his professor.

In a low voice Maston inquired, "What decision are you making?"

DuBose choked out the words,

I hope you'll understand. You see, I've already volunteered for home missions. But in Breckinridge where I'm a pastor, there's a community of Mexican-Americans.

And today I have just realized that I have overlooked these people. We have never tried to reach them for Christ. I know it's not right. We've tried to do some things with the Blacks in our community, but we've just ignored the Mexicans. This morning I've been convicted of my neglect, and I want to put it right. Dr. Maston, you understand what I'm going through—I'm sure you do!

Maston responded, "Yes, Francis, I *do* understand."

He counseled his student further, and they concluded with their own private prayer meeting right there at the front. DuBose pursued a career in home missions that eventually led him to become the professor of missions at the Golden Gate Baptist Seminary.

The matter of white Southern Baptists reaching out to minority groups always struck a responsive cord in Maston's missionary heart. For him there was a basic correlation between right human relationships and missions. During his career as a professor he became a prophet in his denomination. He used his tongue and his pen to stir the conscience of Baptists throughout the South.

One missionary, Peggy Ruble, remembers her first meeting with Maston at a summer conference in the 1950s at Ridgecrest, NC. She was a teenager from the Deep South, brought up understanding that the Black must be kept in "his place." Maston's message about race startled her. She wondered if her ears had garbled the words that had gripped her mind. She waited at the front until she was the last person to shake his hand.

"Did you say," she probed, "that the Bible teaches that if a Negro accepts Christ, he is our brother?"

Gently, he acknowledged, "Yes, that is exactly what the Bible teaches."

It was a new revelation that dawned on the earnest teenager. Later she wrote:

> For me, this previously hidden truth became a seed for thought, which eventually grew into compassion for non-whites, and a Spirit-led compulsion to share the good news of Christ's great love with them. Had he not preached this unpopular concept, I might still be in South Georgia thinking myself righteous by going to church every Sunday.

Cal Guy, a former student and colleague of Maston, had a long and influential career teaching missions at Southwestern. He wrote of Maston's place in the significant interrelationship between race relations and missions,

> Many years ago I heard predictions that Southern Baptists could forget their work in Africa because of the poor record of race relationships here in the United States. Dr. Maston did not change all of those relationships, but he certainly did work at it with great conviction. . . . he helped to initiate some things among Southern Baptists which were desperately needed.

One of the things Maston accomplished in race relations was closer to home. In 1956 he led the faculty to forward a recommendation that prompted the seminary's Board of Trustees to make a signal decision. The board passed a motion to admit blacks to the dormitories and all of the boarding facilities. This virtually eliminated all official discrimination against the black community on campus.

Maston certainly practiced what he taught. Yet what he taught was not so idealistic that it was unworkable. As a master of the possible, he advocated common sense. Frequently, he would illustrate from experiences gained on visits to mission fields. Justice Anderson, professor of missions at Southwestern Seminary, recalls that Maston said in the classroom:

> Now you know I'm an ethics professor, but some of you fellahs are going to need to have some common sense. Now when I go down to Mexico, I'm against bribery, but some times, with the customs of a particular country, you might have to give a little gratification.

Anderson recalls how shocked he and some of his friends were at first. "Some of us guys were so self-righteous, and we were thinking that we were great maximum Christians. . . . but he didn't just come out and approve it." Then Maston would go on about bribery:

> It's not good, but it's part of the system. If you tried to go down there, and the whole time you were in Mexico you just tried to preach against that one practice, you might not ever get anywhere with it. But if you go down and preach the gospel, and the people's hearts are changed, then they are gradually going to try to do something about it.

In this way he guided students to strike a balance. His stance was and is particularly helpful in the missionary situation, where one must work within the realities of the situation at hand.

Maston's rapport with his students was uncanny. He could penetrate into a person's psyche. It is the secret of his ability to understand and to help. Thurmon Bryant relates an extraordinary experience in a graduate seminar. It was at the end of the semester. There were a half dozen students around a table with Maston seated at the end. Maston suggested that he would try to predict the careers of each of the men in that room. He began in clockwise fashion around the table.

"Peter," he said thoughtfully, "you are going to wind up as a denominational writer." He paused, "And you, Bob, you will become an associational missionary." Bryant was next, "Thurmon, you are going to be an administrator."

At that time Bryant wasn't a candidate for missions. His singular goal was simply to be a good pastor. When he heard Maston's prediction, he smiled and thought to himself, *Well, old gentleman, you've missed me because my heart is in the pastorate. I don't see myself as an administrator in the normal sense.*

Within six years, the prediction was fulfilled! Bryant assumed administrative responsibility when Brazilian Baptists along with the missionaries chose him in 1961 as president of the Brazilian Baptist Seminary. Later in Bryant's career, the Foreign Mission Board elected him director for eastern South America.

The twisting kaleidoscope has revealed many designs and colors in Maston's career as a professor. It has presented him fairly as a teacher with a heart for missions. An important dimension of his mission awareness is his family. His wife Essie Mae and their children are such an integral part of whom T. B. Maston is.

Tom Mac

Life greeted Thomas McDonald Maston on November 15, 1925, with an instant permanent injury to his brain. Cerebral damage resulted in lifelong spastic paralysis. On the day of his birth neither parent realized what had happened. T. B. Maston stood in the delivery room and saw Essie Mae go to the brink of death by inches as the infant appeared. He prayed desperately as her body writhed in the anguish of birth. Her survival was uppermost in his mind and heart as she clung to life. She escaped the clutches of death and came back to him. The infant also eluded death, but came through greatly wounded.

The harrowing ordeal was over. Maston, satisfied that his two beloved were safe, went home. He reached their home at 1716 Spurgeon Street. It was an effort to park the car. Trial by birth had racked his emotions. Once in the house he stopped in the dining room, dropped into a chair at the table, and wept. "Why?" he sobbed. "Why did she have to go through such agony and danger?" he groaned.

Maston thought the ordeal was over. It was only beginning. Before long the anxious parents discovered that the child had suffered irreparable paralysis. The diagnosis was cerebral palsy. "Why?" became a shout . . . The birth trauma had dealt the infant son a body out-of-control. They sought expert medical advice in the East. The doctors said, "We do not know anything that can be done for him." It was a soul-shattering verdict.

The experience changed Essie Mae's name to Mommie. That is the affectionate nickname she earned for her constant loving care of the wounded infant. The birth three years later of their second son, Gene, further enhanced the meaning of "Mommie."

Mommie tried diligently to help Tom Mac gain some facility of body movement. He responded like a limp doll. He would not move his hands, arms, feet, or legs. She spent hours on end trying to get him to say something— simple words: *Mommie, Daddy, milk,* and other such everyday things. Her heroic persistence in this painstaking endeavor led to ultimate frustration. He would not— could not—use his body at all. From head to toe he could neither move his voluntary muscles, nor could he say anything.

Finally, Tom Mac's distraught parents reached the heartbreaking conclusion that he was hopelessly dependent. Nevertheless, they determined to make the most of this new life. Severely handicapped though he was, he was God's gift to them. The Lord had entrusted to them the stewardship of this disabled but precious human being.

The birth injury had ravaged Tom Mac's nervous system. With virtually no control of his motor functions he is utterly helpless. Someone must do for him anything essential to everyday life—feed, bathe, shave, comb, brush teeth, dress, undress, put to bed, turn in bed, get up from bed, put into the wheelchair, adjust the straps of the wheelchair—everything.

Throughout most of his life his parents have done everything for him. In later years with an ailing heart, Maston has not been able to do heavy lifting or turning. There is a male attendant from a social service agency who sleeps in his room three nights a week. He turns Tom Mac in bed from two to six times a night. During the rest of the week it is Mommie's task to serve the night watch.

However, Maston remains the one who always sits on Tom Mac's right-hand side and feeds him every bite of food he eats. He *can* swallow. He has a wholesome appetite. Mommie sees to it that her family eats a variety of nutritious food. She cannot omit deserts, however. It's a must on the daily menu.

Sometimes Tom Mac can throw his head upward or sideward in a mass reflex action. Even so his control is minimal. He can move his eyes. And *he can smile!* What a smile! This is his hallmark. His face erupts into the most radiant expression of pleasure in response to the friendly approach of someone who shows interest in him. Tom Mac can also frown. It is a most pitiful grimace. His mood can fluctuate readily from one extreme to the other.

Maston and Mommie have succeeded in working out a minimal means of communication with Tom Mac. He can indicate yes or no in response to simple questions. His yes is a smile while he utters, "Aye." His no is a silent blinking of the eyelids with an accompanying frown. Frequently, he will punctuate the room with an unrestrained howl. It signals either pain, pleasure, or a need of the moment.

Throughout more than six decades of life Tom Mac has enjoyed good health. The common cold brings him far more discomfort than it does to the average person. He cannot clear his throat or blow his nose. He has spent his lifetime in a wheelchair. In spite of this, there is a sense in which he has become a whole person.

Maston insists, "Anyone who has worked closely with Tom Mac will agree that he by nature has a good mind." His inability to read, turn pages, or ask questions has hindered his intellectual development. He gives evidence, however, of a good memory and mental alertness.

Once during his years of active teaching Maston learned that a student, Muriel Waggoner, faced severe financial difficulties. She was on the verge of dropping out of the seminary. The Mastons offered her a job housecleaning on Saturdays. It helped keep her in school. One Saturday she took part in a little episode that demonstrated Tom Mac's quickness of mind.

In those days, men wore garters to hold up their socks. One Saturday morning Maston was missing one of his garters. He searched everywhere for it. Soon Mommie joined in the search. They couldn't find it. They enlisted Muriel's help. The three of them scoured the house hunting for it. Eventually, Tom Mac got into the act.

"Have you seen Daddy's garter, Tom Mac?" Mommie asked. She and Muriel were together in the family room.

"Aye," he replied smilingly.

Mommie and Muriel halted in their tracks and wondered. "Where is it then, Tom Mac? Is it in this room?" asked Mommie.

"Aye," he said. The two ransacked the family room until Muriel gave up and went into the kitchen.

Mommie was exasperated. She sighed, "Tom Mac, I don't think it's in here." He frowned. She persisted, "Tell me now, is it in the dining room?"

Blinking eyes said no.

Maston joined the game, "Tom Mac, is it in the kitchen?"

Quickly, his face opened into a smile as he uttered, "Aye."

"Oh, Tom Mac, you're just teasin' us," retorted Mommie. "Muriel," she called, "do you see it in the kitchen? Tom Mac says it's in there."

Muriel came into the family room. "Pardon, Ma'am?" she said, "I didn't hear what you said."

"There it is," said the professor. "It's hooked on the back of Muriel's dress!" She was wearing an eyelet dress peppered with small holes. The garter had snagged in one of the holes and followed her everywhere she went.

"Well I'll be!" exclaimed Mommie as she reached down and plucked the errant garter. "Tom Mac was right all the time. He wasn't teasin' us after all."

"That's right," chimed in Maston. "Wherever she was, the garter was on her dress, and Tom Mac knew it. Mommie, he's got better eyes than we do."

The room burst into laughter. Muriel looked at Tom Mac. He beamed one of his trademark smiles.

Mommie describes her oldest son in glowing terms,

Tom Mac is a pretty happy person, if he is well, and if you can get him comfortable, unless they get the straps [on the wheelchair] too tight . . . He enjoys life! He has his own programs that he likes to watch [on television], and when it's time to change, why, he'll let you know. He hollers . . . I learned that he likes the old programs . . . "Little House on the Prairie" . . . Someone will ask, "Did you see that program last night?" And I say, "No, all we see are Tom Mac's programs!" . . . He likes to go out. Used to, every Sunday afternoon we'd take him on a long drive, 'specially in the spring when flowers are blooming.

When the weather allows, they all go to church together. It is only a stone's throw from their home to the Gambrell Street Baptist Church on the same avenue. A deacon comes to roll Tom Mac in the wheelchair. They take up their customary station at the very back of the church on the left-hand side facing the pulpit. Tom Mac is always pleased when members come to greet him.

Maston once wrote, "It may be unfair to speak of him as a burden at all. There are things about him that add joy to our lives." He reflects on Tom Mac's interest in life, "He loves the outdoors and likes to sit in the yard in his chair and 'watch the world go by.' . . . He's a good traveler, too . . . seen more of the world than most people."

When someone broached the question of Tom Mac's spiritual condition, Maston replied earnestly:

I trust him to the Lord. Now, let's put it like that. I have not pushed Tom Mac on a decision because I don't think I should. But I do know that he likes to go to church. . . . I personally have no question about Tom Mac. But we have never tried to push him and say, "Now Tom Mac, do you believe and so forth." Now, wisely or unwisely, that's been our position. . . . We've never considered baptism because it isn't essential . . . I have no question about Tom Mac's relationship to the Lord, and I don't think Mommie has either.

On the afternoon of November 28, 1986, two days after Maston's eighty-ninth birthday, I visited in the Maston home. We sat in the little breakfast nook talking quietly. Since Mommie was not yet up from her daily nap, we didn't want to disturb her by going into the family room. Around four o'clock Robert Flowers, the seminary student on duty, wheeled Tom Mac into the room. He had just awakened from his nap. Robert had washed his face and combed his hair neatly. Tom Mac transmitted his signature smile as he entered. Maston reached out to take Tom Mac's right hand in his. With hands joined, the father began speaking to his son in soft affectionate tones. He then turned to his guest and began to brag on his son, "Can you imagine? Tom Mac has stayed contentedly for sixty-one years in a wheelchair!" Maston emphasized, "Now, that's something!"

Pure joy radiated from Tom Mac's face. Any temptation to pity either Tom Mac or his family evaporated. In that moment one could sense a flow of love passing between them through their hands. Love evoked that unforgettable smile.

Someone who didn't know any better might think the Mastons' had only one son. To be sure, Tom Mac is the only offspring residing in the Maston home. There is another son, one less often seen, who fits admirably into the missionary pilgrimage of the Maston family.

Gene

Harold Eugene Maston, better known as "Gene," lives in New York City. He is a teacher cum tour guide in the famous metropolis. The urban scene appeals to Gene's dynamic sense of mission. He gained access to the city by successfully exchanging his identity from intruder to insider. His journey begs to be told.

The excursion begins with the courage of Maston and Mommie after the birth of Tom Mac. With the trauma of that life-threatening experience fresh in their memories, they determined to have another child. They accepted the assurance that a cesarean section would remove most of the potential danger and injury of the first delivery.

On August 30, 1928, almost three years after the birth of Tom Mac, Mommie gave life to another son, Gene. In spite of assurances to the contrary, it brought her once again to the brink of death. For a second time she survived. The delivery avoided injury to the infant. In the ensuing months, the couple decided against having any more children. They reasoned, "It was better to have a live mother with two children than to have more children and have to bring them up as orphans."

In his growing years, Gene was as impressionable as any normal boy. A home built on love afforded him a favorable environment for interest in things Christian. His intellect developed out of hearty curiosity. He learned how to read well early in life. His appetite for things to read challenged the resources of the house. *National Geographic* magazines were a favorite. In devouring them he cultivated a fascination for faraway places. When he reached adulthood, Mommie taunted him that the *National Geographic* subscription may have been a mistake. She teased that reading those magazines gave him an itching for foreign lands.

His parents' wide circle of friendships brought a long line of visitors to the home. The majority of the guests were furloughing missionaries. Maston hospitality furnished the lad the chance to get acquainted with many missionary valiants. There was Blanche Groves, the faithful correspondent, and Helen McCullough. Both were serving in China. Charles and Ola Culpepper (Sr.) who were also from China visited from time to time. They had been fellow seminary students with the Mastons. Anne Laseter, missionary to Chile, likewise, had been close to them during student years. These along with many others gave Gene some ready-made heros to idolize.

Gene's attraction toward missions emerged naturally in a home where missions and missionaries were regular agenda. Of course, influences at church added to his mission awareness. His parents never consciously urged missions on him. He explains, "A lot of times you pick up things from the air you breathe." One scarcely can imagine a home providing such an atmosphere for missions that a child would constantly inhale it into his system. This was missionary zeal by osmosis.

Student years at Baylor University encouraged a continuing motivation for missions. In the summer of 1947, Gene followed his parents' example of summer missions. He worked among American Baptist churches in Kansas. The earliest efforts of sending student teams to mission projects overseas during the summer break impressed Gene. The first team went to Hawaii. Later others went to Latin America.

Gene enrolled at Southwestern Seminary in pursuit of God's direction for his life. During his first semester, he learned about an eight-day preaching mission to the Bahamas in the summer just past. Several pastors from Oklahoma had engaged in the project. They reported hundreds who had professed Christ. It aroused Gene's interest. He wrote to Guy Bellamy of the Home Mission Board, SBC, who had led the team. Gene proposed that a team of seminary students do a project in the Bahamas during the summer of 1950. His proposal met with immediate favor.

He sought the advice of the missions professor, Cal Guy. The professor gave positive encouragement, counseling the enlistment of a faculty member to lead the team. Gene approached another professor, Jack MacGorman. The student went into the young professor's office waving a copy of the March, 1950, issue of the *Southern Baptist Home Missions* magazine. It motivated Jack and his wife, Ruth, to accept. "There I was," remembers MacGorman, "a rookie teacher leading the students."

The Bahamas project fired the interest of the Mission Band, a student organization of mission volunteers. Along with Gene and the MacGormans the team needed more personnel. Ted and Jean Thompson, Harold Wells, and Wimpy Smith agreed to participate in the twelve-week program.

The group went prepared to conduct Vacation Bible Schools on the islands of New Providence, Andros, and

Eluthera. Opportunities to preach came also. They discovered the Baptists of the islands in deep turmoil. They were bitterly divided among a half dozen associations. There were several Baptist dictatorships of sorts. The Baptist groups ranged in the worship spectrum from the sedate minority influenced mainly by British Baptists to the charismatic "Jumpers." Many of the leaders were more interested in siphoning off Southern Baptist money than in developing the educational work of the churches.

Gene exclaims, "We were 'Innocents Abroad.'" He calls it ". . . one of the most stressful summers I have ever spent . . . it was a real pressure cooker." However, his concluding assessment is, "I have always felt that whatever the difficulties, it was God's will for us to be there."

The team carried out the program regardless of problems. They found young people and adults who were eager to learn. The urgent need for leadership training impressed the Americans. They grew convinced that the islands required more than short-term help.

One evening Gene was strolling with a young Bahamian Baptist along the market wharf in Nassau. It was deep dusk. The many one-masted sloops in the harbor appeared as ghostly silhouettes. Voices floated across the water. Gene said to his companion, "Am I hearing some boatmen talking in French?"

"Yes, of course," came the rely. "Those boats are not just from the Bahamas. They come from Haiti, Cuba, and the Lesser Antilles."

"I see," said Gene. He nodded his head thoughtfully.

During the remainder of his stay in Nassau, Gene spent

his spare time in the city library. He researched thoroughly the other islands in the West Indies archipelago. He was
preparing to make an intelligent appeal for Southern Baptists to instigate mission work on the islands.

After the project was over and they had returned to the
Southwestern campus, a determined Gene persisted in
making a full report to all concerned. He and Jack Mac-
Gorman sent in separate reports to the Southern Baptist
Foreign Mission Board. They explained in detail the situation in the Bahamas and outlined what the team had
accomplished. Both urged favorable consideration for
long-range Southern Baptist work in the Bahamas and in
the other islands of the West Indies.

Sometime during the 1950-51 academic year, Everett
Gill, Jr., secretary for Latin America for the Foreign Mission Board, visited the campus. Gene arranged an appointment with him. Their session became a debate. Gene
carefully laid out the data, reinforcing it with his personal
sense of urgency. Gill was unmoved as he marshaled the
reasons for the Board's inability to take on such new work.
He resisted the gritty presentation of the upstart seminari-
an. It was a stalemate. Gene left the conference forlorn.
He thought he had failed.

To his astonishment, soon after their meeting Gene
learned that the Foreign Mission Board had entered the
work in the Bahamas! In that very same year, 1951, the
Board deployed a veteran missionary couple to serve as
fraternal representatives. In 1953 a second couple joined
the work. Immediately, they established the Baptist Bible

Institute. The vision that Gene, MacGorman, and company had seen became a reality.

In a chapel service at Southwestern Seminary in 1973, Baptists from the Bahamas honored Gene for his part in the beginning of Southern Baptist involvement in the West Indies. The Baptist Mission of the Bahamas along with the Bahamas Baptist Missionary and Educational Convention presented him with a plaque. They gave tribute to his role in instigating the Bahamas Summer Missions Program. It was significant as the first of a series of summer projects to the islands sponsored by Southwestern students for many years.

Gene went to the Bahamas to test his commitment to overseas missions. It was clearly one of his reasons for going. Earnestly, he prayed that he might perceive a sense of divine leadership. He sorely wanted to clarify the direction of his vocation. Years later he reflects, "It was a case where I wanted—really wanted—to go into mission work overseas but could never feel that the Lord was leading me to do it." Missionary zeal by osmosis is never enough!

Health problems also rendered an effective deterrent to missionary service. During his undergraduate years, Gene fell ill with rheumatic fever. It induced a lingering arthritis. Later when he reached the age of twenty-eight, diabetes sealed the door completely against overseas service. The diagnosis labelled it as diabetes of the uncommon "brittle" variety.

Upon graduation from seminary, Gene plunged into a different kind of mission field. It is one often hidden from the eyes of unsuspecting church members. The student generation evokes a perennial call to evangelize and to minister. It is indeed a distinct culture. Gene sensed within himself a new direction in missions when he entered the campus ministry at McNeese State College, Lake Charles, Louisiana. His work tested, proved, and prepared him for pioneer student work in Southern Baptists' new areas.

Gene Bolin, pastor of the Metro Baptist Church, New York City, calls Gene Maston, "The father of Baptist student work in Chicago, New York City, and the whole Northeast." Gene resigned from his work at McNeese State to begin graduate studies at the University of Chicago in the fall of 1957. On his own initiative, he made a thorough survey of existing student work in the metropolitan area. His report included recommendations for meeting the needs. The recommendations faltered. However, within a year, single-handedly he founded a student ministry at the University of Chicago.

Gene transferred his graduate work to Columbia University in New York City in 1959. An earlier interest in previous work on the campus of Princeton University was still on his mind and heart. He revisited the Princeton campus and found that continued sponsorship for a Baptist group proved unfeasible. Immediately, he set his focus on the New York metropolitan area. Once again he performed a thorough survey and prepared a comprehensive forty-four-page report. The needs of the city's student population stirred Gene to write in his report:

> Literally thousands of students are unreached by any Protestant ministry, whether evangelical or not. If we take

seriously the Great Commission, we must, so far as possible, reach these students as surely as we seek to reach the primitive tribes of Africa. More blind than the African, these students hear and speak the name of Christ in a quasi-Christian society without ever grasping its real significance.

The report met with approval in the Manhattan Baptist Church and in the Northeastern Baptist Association. The formation of a Sunday School class for university students marked the birth of student work in the area. Gene taught the class. Eventually, out of the nucleus provided by his class, there evolved a separate student group for the entire New York City area in early 1960. It embraced students who were already active in other churches or missions. It was the first student ministry for Southern Baptists in the northeastern United States.

In the spring of 1961 the Maryland Baptist Convention with the Sunday School Board engaged Gene as full-time student director for the northeastern region. During the next seven-and-one-half years, Gene was the prime mover in founding student ministries on the following campuses: the United States Military Academy at West Point, Harvard University, Massachusetts Institute of Technology, the United States Coast Guard Academy, and Yale University.

He was also instrumental along with others in establishing groups at Vassar College, University of Syracuse, and the United States Merchant Marine Academy. Poor health compelled Gene to resign in the summer of 1968.

At the time there were seven groups actively meeting in the greater New York area. One of these was a ministry to international students.

Gene paid a high price for his activities in starting the various campus organizations. The extensive undertaking demanded all of his time and concentration. He neglected the graduate program. Eventually, he abandoned it altogether. Since the time of his resignation from student work, Gene has not felt the motivation to resume graduate studies.

On the denominational level, Gene served as a goad, prodding for the support of campus ministries in new areas. He attended meetings, corresponded, and wrote articles to carry out his campaign. In recalling his role at this level he grants, "I was simply an informational source or a gadfly, depending on one's point of view."

There's significance in the birth of the first Southern Baptist student work in New York City. The womb that produced it was a local church. There is no surprise in this when one realizes Gene inherited from his parents an undying devotion to the church.

Gene has expressed his missionary drive through the activities of a local congregation. Upon his arrival in New York City, he entered the life of the Manhattan Baptist Church. Soon his church gave him responsibility for leadership as chairman of the Missions Committee. Mission chapels already begun were nurtured. Gene also led the church to begin new work in the Borough of Queens and on Staten Island.

In the late sixties, a change of pastoral leadership

proved disastrous for the Manhattan Baptist Church. Gene watched helplessly as the congregation changed priorities. Its missionary outreach became defunct. Gradually, attendance dwindled until the church held no hope for survival. At the same time, Gene was chronically ill. Also he was experiencing severe personal problems. His active participation in the church abated for several years.

A remnant from the abandoned Manhattan Church persuaded Gene to join them in beginning anew. He had recovered somewhat from his illness and was himself ready for a new beginning. The nucleus launched a week-night Bible study group. Within months in the summer of 1974, a mission chapel evolved. Eventually, it constituted as the Metro Baptist Church.

Gene has served a multisplendored role in that church. The catalog of his active responsibilities includes: Sunday School teacher, usher, and deacon. He has held the chairmanship of the Pastor Search Committee, the Missions Committee, and more recently been Chairman of the Deacons.

Through Gene's leadership, the church has adopted the struggling Park Slope Baptist Chapel in Brooklyn. He started a Portuguese mission. In addition he has conducted a ministry to the street kids in the church's neighborhood. He instigated the church's involvement in the Ninth Avenue International Food Fair in the spring of 1986. In this event, the church along with the help of a team from a Texas church gave out fifteen- to twenty-thousand cups of cold water to the public in Jesus' name. At the same time they also gave out Scripture portions. Similarly, the church entered the celebration of "Freedom 86," the centennial of the Statue of Liberty, at South Battery Park. There they distributed twenty-four-thousand "Jesus" books.

Ministering among minorities is a priority that has excited Gene's attention. He has invested much time and energy in this direction. His influence has inspired many to follow the Christian way. Gene prefers to work with persons individually. His personal ministry gravitates mostly toward blacks. He considers this work with minorities to be the fulfillment of his earlier missionary vision. ". . . this is likely the kind of contribution I would have made had I gone overseas." he asserts, continuing, "So in a way I have been on mission."

A visit to the Metro Baptist Church in 1987 during the Sunday activities impressed Thurman Bryant of the Foreign Mission Board, SBC staff. He observed appreciatively Gene's involvement in the church's missionary outreach. Bryant concludes, "What Gene is doing in New York City is as difficult as any mission work I have witnessed overseas."

His father agrees that Gene's life and work in New York City are definitely a missionary situation. Maston remembers a conversation he had with his son on a visit there.

Now the thing that I've said to him half-jokingly but pretty serious, I said, 'I'd have to have a special divine revelation to come up here and live here.' But this is what he has always said to me, 'But Daddy, this is where the people are.'

Gene has become an urban missionary. His parents are grateful for what God has done through his life and ministry in the city. Maston pronounces approval in his words, "We are proud of him. He has had some rough experiences in life but he has, so far as we know, come through them in good shape." The excursion into the life of son Gene reflects the missionary burden of his parents, and now the story of that burden must continue.

First Pilgrimage

Servant-pilgrim T. B. Maston embarked on his first missionary odyssey in 1954. A resolute longing to see former students motivated him. Seven years before, Mommie had traveled to a Baptist World Alliance meeting in Europe. She had urged him to attend the next scheduled meeting in 1955. Yearning to see missionaries in action, Maston declined in favor of a trip to Latin America.

Already he had made several forays into Mexico. There he discovered that he could minister among missionaries in mission meetings. In the Mexican pastors' meetings, Maston learned that lecturing through an interpreter could be effective. Such experiences whetted his appetite for more.

Therefore, Maston proposed a grand tour of Central and South America. It was a pioneer idea for his generation of theological professors. Of course, one could find ample precedent in the New Testament. The apostle Paul, a converted rabbi, theologian, and itinerant missionary, circulated among the churches he had established. The record reads that Paul "traveled from place to place

throughout the region . . . strengthening all the disciples
. . . he was a great help to those who by grace had believed" (Acts 18:23,27*b*, NIV). Maston fitted the precedent even though he never established a single church. His
students, however, as the extension of his missionary burden, evangelized and started many churches. Therefore,
he would travel to visit the missionaries and to strengthen
the believers.

It was a case of volunteering. No one gave Maston an
assignment to go. To be sure, the missionaries had invited
him repeatedly. It was a standing invitation. Maston
seized the opportunity and set the plans in motion. He
suggested the journey to Everett Gill, Jr., the Foreign
Mission Board's area secretary for Latin America. Active
correspondence during the ensuing months settled the
itinerary.

Notwithstanding his great desire for the trip, Maston
experienced some natural misgivings as the date for departure approached. For one thing, leaving the care for Tom
Mac with Mommie concerned him. For another, the itinerary itself promised to be strenuous for him. Out of eight
full weeks, only one was unscheduled and free of lecturing.
It would tax both his physical strength and mental resources.

There arose another consideration six days before departure. Gill's secretary, Thelma Bryant, called from
Richmond, Virginia, to ask if Maston would carry an item
to one of the missionaries. After giving his consent, they
discussed the volatile situation in Latin America. Revolution was in the air. Paraguay had already been cut from

the schedule because of a revolutionary conflict. Miss Bryant suggested that Maston consider the omission of Guatemala and Honduras also. Maston was undaunted.

Since it was a volunteer venture, the Mastons dug into their meager savings to fund the trip. On the day before his departure, Charles Johnson, one of Maston's graduate students, appeared at the door of their home. He handed the professor a check for four-hundred dollars. Johnson informed him that his graduate students had taken up an offering to help with the cost of the journey. Even the seminary's president, J. Howard Williams, had heard about it and added his contribution to the purse. Later donations brought the total to more than five-hundred dollars. It overwhelmed the Mastons.

Two months later upon completion of his travels, Maston sent a copy of his report to those who had contributed. To one of those who represented the ethics majors he wrote,

> We did not expect any help from any source and were surprised . . . I want each of you to know, whether you gave anything or not and regardless of how little or how much you might have given, that I count you as one of my own.

Maston had expressed the hope in letters to former students in Latin America that his visits would not be a bother. Ruben Franks replied from Chile, "Don't feel that you will be a bother to us . . . You will be 'the shot in the arm' that we have been needing." The assurance spurred Maston on. He wrote another missionary, "I think the thing I look forward to more than anything else is the fellowship that I will have with you folks and with many others who have been former students.

Maston flew into Guatemala on the heels of the latest revolution. It was the first Pan American flight after the reopening of the airport. The missionaries determined to proceed with the four-day pastors' conference. One pastor had to walk sixteen miles to Guatemala City because insurgents had blown up the railroad near his village.

The tour started like a whirlwind. An overnight stopover in Honduras allowed for only one pastors' meeting. Maston learned from the missionaries that theirs was the most pioneer work in Latin America. There were only twelve miles of paved roads. The literacy rate was 15 percent. The work was progressing rapidly. They had constituted three churches. Already there were thirty mission chapels.

Onward Maston traveled to Costa Rica. The sight of familiar faces among the missionaries that greeted him at the airport in San Jose cheered him. During the first afternoon, one of the missionaries, Clark Scanlon, took him on a tour of the city and its environs. They stopped to climb Irazu, an active volcanic mountain near Caratago. Scanlon remembers Maston's zest for life as they climbed toward the summit. Maston posed for a picture in his topcoat with tousled hair blowing in the wind.

The theme for the conference of pastors and missionaries was "The Christian Home." During a break in the schedule, missionary Charles Bryan took Maston to see the Guadalupe Baptist Church. The congregation had grown from five to one hundred in a short time and had started another mission chapel in the first four years of its existence.

The immediate scene introduced Maston to the typical Latin American situation of an overwhelming Roman Catholic presence. He observed a sign placed across the street from the church. Bryan translated it, "We reverence Christ, We love the Virgin Mary, We obey the Pope."

Not only did Maston learn much on his trip but also he was able to help many missionaries and nationals along the way. Later in life he reflected on this particular journey. He considered that it was well that he went alone. Accommodation in the homes of missionaries afforded him excellent opportunities to minister. In the relaxed situation of a home they felt freer to open up to him. One missionary recalls that he became, "a 'Father Confessor' to all of us!"

Maston's stay with Charles and Martha Bryan was like being with old friends. Three years earlier, when they had returned to the States after language school, they sought his counsel. At the time they had been married three years with no sign of having children. They wondered about the advisability of adoption as an alternative. Maston counseled them not to give up yet on having their own but to wait. Their first child, Carol Ann, was born two years later in 1953.

Without grandchildren of his own, Maston immediately assumed the grandfather role. He often romped with the fourteen-month-old toddler on the living room floor. Every evening she would rush into his arms at bedtime to kiss him goodnight. They became well attached. Once when she had misbehaved Charles started to spank her. Maston reached out his hand to restrain him saying, "Wait a minute—not right now—please—just don't do it now." Once again a grandfather engineered the sparing of the rod!

Clark Scanlon tells of Maston as mediator. Two missionary couples were having serious interpersonal conflict. Though no one had mentioned it, Maston sensed that something was wrong between them. Maston drew them out. He helped them to bring it into the open and to discuss it. The healing of broken relationships and the resolution of some problems resulted.

Martha Bryan wrote a warm personal letter to Mommie the day after his departure from Costa Rica. She expressed their deep appreciation for Mommie's unselfishness in encouraging Maston's travels and for staying home with Tom Mac. Martha reported that he had shown signs at times of being, "a wee bit homesick." She assured Mommie that although he worked a busy schedule, he managed to get a siesta every afternoon.

Martha called him, "the perfect house guest." Her letter tells of one instance when she went to his room to call him to breakfast. As he came out of the room to go down the steps he stopped abruptly, did an about-face, and returned to the room. He said, "Mrs. Maston is always getting after me about leaving the closet door open." He closed the door and wore a smile. Martha called it, "the smuggest grin of satisfaction on his face, I've ever seen."

His odyssey took him next to the Panama Canal Zone.

There he paid a two-day visit to the serviceman son of old friends from Fort Worth. He also saw some of the Baptist work of the Home Mission Board of the Southern Baptist Convention.

Maston's next hop took him to Colombia. A week free of lecturing gave him the opportunity to enjoy a motor tour through the Colombian countryside. His idea of sight-seeing was to visit the Baptist work in as many places as possible. Missionary Zack Deal was his guide. Deal came from Cartagena, where he resided, to meet Maston's flight at Barrauquilla. They first went around Barrauquilla to see some of the churches, a clinic, and a youth camp. Then they set out for Cartagena.

En route, Maston enjoyed the rural scenery. He marveled at the men traveling on burros from their farms into town to sell their produce. He saw a container strapped to one of the animals. Maston asked the missionary, "What is that burro carrying?"

"Water," replied Deal.

"Do you mean to tell me that he's taking water into town?" the professor remarked.

"It's true," said the missionary. Deal continued, "He got that water from the lake that we just passed."

"You mean the lake where we just saw women washing their clothes? And there were burros standing in the same water?" Maston exclaimed incredulously.

"That's exactly right," asserted Deal, adding jestingly, "There's a premium on that water in town because it's greatly enriched!"

On the return trip to Barrauquilla, they encountered a

T. B. Maston (right) with his brother Red (left)
and sister Nora (center).

An early Maston family portrait: (from left) Tom, Tom Mac, Gene, Mommie. (Photo by Frank Simpson)

On mission trip to Argentina: Mommie, T. B., Tom Mac, and José Pistones, secretary-treasurer of International Baptist Theological Seminary, Buenos Aires, in faculty lounge.

The Mastons with silver serving tray presented when he retired from teaching at Southwestern Baptist Theological Seminary.

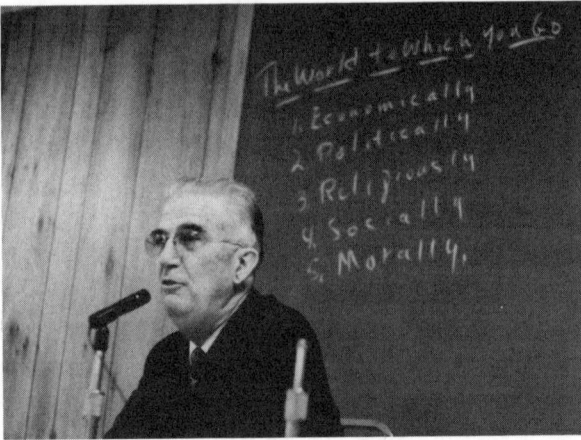

Maston lecturing at the Foreign Mission Board's career orientation center at Callaway Gardens, Pine Mountain, Georgia, September, 1971. (FMB Photo by W. Robert Hart)

Maston at the dedication of the Missionary Learning Center in Rockville, Virginia, October, 1984, with (left) Dr. Louis R. Cobbs, Director of the Foreign Mission Board's Personnel Selection Department and (right) Weston Ware of the Baptist General Convention of Texas. (FMB Photo by Warren Johnson)

Mommie.

Gene.

Maston in his office at Southwestern.

Maston with the author (right) on the
Southwestern Seminary campus.

rain shower. The missionary stopped his car. Maston wondered what was wrong—*Did the engine drown out so quickly?* he thought. Deal reached his hand in back of the front seat of the station wagon and pulled out two windshield wiper blades. "Why do you keep them there?" Maston inquired.

"That's so they won't be lifted when we park it," said Deal as he fitted the blades onto the wiper arms.

"I'm learnin' a lot today," chuckled the professor with a broad smile.

When Maston left for Bogota he understood better how missionaries cope in a Latin culture. During a two-day visit to Bogota he continued visiting with missionaries and saw more of the churches. He was gathering missionary intelligence day by day.

Maston's arrival in Cali, Colombia, signalled a return to speaking and lecturing in conferences and seminary classrooms. A novel experience greeted him. The missionaries introduced him to the two-wheel mode of missionary transportation. One of the missionaries used a motorcycle. Another, Hoke Smith, tooled all over the city in a motor scooter. Maston's preference was the scooter. It was much tamer. With Hoke in the saddle the professor would mount the second seat over the rear wheel and off they sped. Maston learned how to hold tightly to the grip handle on the back of the first seat. Then he would squeeze his legs around the rear-wheel housing to stay on when they turned corners. Riding with Hoke provided some thrills he hadn't counted on.

Continuing southward from Colombia he landed in

Quito, Ecuador. The missionaries greeted him warmly and handed him a batch of letters from Mommie. His first opportunity to read them came when they reached the missionary's home. The letters informed him vividly about the Texas heat wave. Mommie wrote,

> Dear Daddy, You should be glad you got away from Texas when you did, for it has turned on the heat good now. . . . It was 103 the day you left and has been above 100 every day since. I'll give you our temperatures for the past week and if you are where it is cold this will serve as a portable heater for you . . . so don't ever feel cold when you get where it is cold.

He burst out laughing. Gleefully he shared the news with his hosts.

They told him that the city was only fifteen miles from the equator. Yet it was cold. At ninety-five-hundred feet altitude, the night air demanded a fire in the fireplace. At bedtime Maston snuggled under an electric blanket and thought about Mommie's letters. He determined to take her suggestion and try not to feel the cold.

He proceeded the next day by plane to Guayaquil, Ecuador, for three days of conferences. Again there was time to see some of the churches and to be with missionaries. When he left on the flight to Lima, Peru, he passed the halfway mark in the eight-week journey.

The flight stopped briefly at La Paz, Bolivia. At more than twelve-thousand feet it boasts the highest airport in the world. He took pictures of the snow-capped Andes in the background. After takeoff when the plane was airborne once again, it nosed in a southerly direction toward Chile.

Anne Laseter greeted him at Santiago's airport with a typical Latin *abrazo*—a wholehearted hug. Since they had been friends for more than thirty years, Anne felt she'd earned the right to a warm embrace. Later when he returned to Fort Worth, Maston exclaimed, "I've never been hugged and kissed as much in my life. I suppose the missionary women see in me a father figure, and a link with home."

Maston remembers Santiago as the most beautiful place of all of the cities he saw on the tour. A fresh snowfall on the day before his arrival provided a white blanket on the surrounding mountains. Newly formed ice every morning made him appreciate the cold by contrast to the torrid Texas summer reported in Mommie's letters.

The missionaries took him to the top of Mount Cristobal overlooking the city. He gazed in wonder at the shrine that dominates the crest of the mountain. There is a large crucifix flanked by two crosses. Both figures on the crosses are women. Above the crosses at the highest point of the summit there is a much larger statue of the virgin Mary. Only the image of Mary is illuminated at night. To his companions, Maston offered his personal conclusion: "A dead Christ overshadowed by Mary." To himself he considered that it was "symbolic of one thing that is wrong with Latin America."

Maston's next flight was a literal turning point in the Latin American circuit. The plane carried him due east across the majestic Andes to Buenos Aires. After four days of conferences, he skipped in hopscotch fashion to Montevideo, Uruguay, for yet another series of meetings.

At the beginning of the seventh week he flew to Rio de Janeiro. It pleased him to learn upon arrival that he would stay in the home of missionaries Edgar and Zelma Hallock. Edgar's father was an outstanding pastor in Oklahoma with whom Maston was well acquainted. Before he left on the trip Maston had known about Edgar's reputation for being an excellent missionary.

They reached the missionary home late at night. The hosts spared their travel-weary guest the inconvenience of extended conversation and suggested that he might want to go to bed. When he entered the room he saw a pile of letters on the dresser. Immediately he snatched them up and sorted the ones from Mommie. Eagerly he tore into them and sitting on the edge of the bed began to read. The flaming heat of July had continued into August. Mommie lamented the loss of two pullets even though she had watered the pen to cool the chickens. On the second of August she wrote, "We are enjoying cool ninety-six-degree weather."

A wave of homesickness washed over him as she shared about local things, "Picked the last of the figs this morning. Have made fourteen pints of preserves." The revival services at the church were, "rather matter of fact . . . nothing spectacular." Her letter of August fourth states casually, "Suppose we are at the halfway mark of this marital vacation now. Will be glad to get the family together again." It was a remarkable understatement. Maston reciprocated the sentiment. He went to sleep that night with Mommie's words lingering in his heart. In two more weeks the family would indeed be together again.

He spoke and lectured at the customary meetings at the Baptist Seminary and in the churches. Hallock was his interpreter for every occasion. Maston observed that the missionary was especially well loved and respected." There must be a secret to his effectiveness," he thought. He wondered what it was. Soon he would learn.

One afternoon Maston and Hallock were invited to accompany a group of students of the Women's Missionary Union Training School for a weekly mission activity. It was a ministry of outreach in a slum area near the school in the hilly outskirts of the city. As the group climbed a hill, children came out of their hovels. When they recognized that it was the young women, they gleefully ran alongside the escorting them to the top of the hill. They spotted the *americanos* immediately.

Maston observed the children as they went into the meeting place. Some of the children were white skinned. The rest were varying shades of brown. Some were clean; others came unwashed. The young women conducted the service while the two men sat observing. At the end of the service Hallock, on behalf of his guest, thoughtfully suggested that the children line up outside the building. This would give the professor a chance to take a picture of the group.

While children were gathering for the picture, two of them came to Hallock to say something. He hunkered down to be on their level. Then he put his right arm around a child who was dark skinned. Some of the color was probably dirt. Likewise, his left arm closed around the other child of the slum.

The missionary listened intently as the children spoke to him. As Maston looked on, suddenly he discovered the answer to Hallock's effectiveness. "That's the secret!" Maston thrilled within himself, "He loves people regardless of age, color, or condition of life."

Latin America provides the stranger with a macrocosm of humanity. Among many of its qualities, it exudes the warmth of cordiality. In Brazil, a noteworthy episode impressed Maston regarding Latin courtesy and generosity.

From Rio he took an internal flight to Sao Paulo. He was a day later than the missionary Rodney Wolfard expected. There was no one at the airport to meet him. In the event such a thing might happen, Wolfard had given Maston specific instructions about his onward bus journey to Campinas.

Maston found his way to the taxi stand to try to get a ride to the bus station. Without knowing any Portuguese, he felt very vulnerable. At this point Maston picks up the story in his own words:

A white-headed Brazilian, who could not speak English, understood the predicament I was in. I showed him the card [containing Wolfard's instructions], he pointed to the taxicab and in some way communicated to me that he was going to the bus station. When I started to pay the red cap . . . he waved a finger—which meant no—and gave him a tip. When we got to the bus station and got out of the taxicab, I started to get out my purse and pay the taxi driver, and again he waved no and paid the driver. He took me to the bus station to the right window . . . and after I bought the ticket, he motioned to me to come back to a place where we could get a bite to eat. I took out my purse again to pay for the light lunch we had, he waved a finger again saying no and paid for that. Then he took me out to the front to one of the red caps . . . and I could tell he was telling him what bus I was to catch and that I could not speak any Portuguese. Then, he pointed to my bags, gave the fellow a tip, shook my hand, and left.

The experience represents only one of several occasions when he benefitted much from Latin friendliness.

The homing instinct was growing stronger within him. Following his side-trips in South Brazil he flew northward to Recife, North Brazil. After a week with the missionaries and Brazilian Baptists, he proceeded homeward with a one-day stop at Belem in equatorial Brazil.

On the next to last day of August he started on the last leg of his long journey. His return trip required a series of three hops on three different airlines for a duration of thirty-three hours.

When Maston walked into his home at 4400 James Avenue, Fort Worth, he was greeted with royal smiles by both Mommie and Tom Mac. Indeed the family was back "together again."

He had covered a lot of territory in the eight-week span. He slept a night or more in twenty cities in ten different countries plus the Panama Canal Zone. On all but two of the fifty-seven nights he slept in a home with missionaries. Maston saw 147 Southern Baptist missionaries. Over half of them were former students of his. It was a memorable pilgrimage.

Among the letters that Maston received following the journey was an especially poignant one. Significantly, it came from a black Columbian pastor, Ramon Pacheco, who attended the conferences in Cali. He had wanted to express his thanks before the group at the close of the meetings. However, someone else was chosen to be the spokesperson.

In Spanish, Pacheco expressed his gratitude for Maston's lectures. He explained that the messages "awakened in me a greater commitment to the work of the Lord." He called Maston "an ambassador of good will." The pastor went on heaping many words of admiration on the professor.

> it is so infrequent to find among the people who visit us, especially here in Columbia, the kind of rapport that we have had with you . . . I don't consider you a stranger.

The last sentence is probably one of the highest compliments a mission traveler could expect.

The odyssey was only the first of several missionary journeys. Nor was this the last time Maston would be complimented for his instant rapport and durable influence on individuals wherever he went.

Orient Retreats

Was the passenger on the military aircraft dressed in civilian clothes Major General T. B. Maston, US Army?

If not an officer, how did he manage to receive the treatment for such rank without joining the army? Before departure at Travis Air Force Base, his baggage was labelled VIP. As a passenger he was among the first to board and deplane. He sat in the section reserved for ranking officers, the section that receives priority during meal service.

The above describes Maston's transpacific flight to the Orient on a United States Air Force plane on October 21, 1959. His presence on the flight probably stimulated such thoughts in the minds of fellow passengers. He, himself, wondered about traveling in such style. The situation was most undemocratic but very military!

Maston was on a mission for Major General Frank A. Tobey, United States Army chief of chaplains. Accordingly, the VIP status came from the Pentagon. One of Maston's former students, Colonel Wallace Hale, had recommended the professor to Tobey for the 1959 chaplains' retreats in the Orient. Tobey issued an invitation. Maston accepted. Consequently, he was flying to the Orient as the "retreat master."

The retreats offered a theological refresher for the chaplains. Tobey explained that Protestant chaplains of all branches of the United States armed forces would attend. The conglomeration of Protestant traditions at the retreats posed a formidable challenge to Maston. It was his first experience lecturing to groups with a majority of non-Baptists. He was anxious about the reaction a mixed group would give to his lectures. Nevertheless, he determined, "I'm going to do exactly what I would do if I were talking to a bunch of Baptists." This he did with considerable success.

The twenty-eight-day tour began with his departure from Texas on October 21, 1959, and ended with his return on November 18. It carried Maston to military bases in three countries of the Orient. Five-day retreats were staged in South Korea: October 26-30; Japan: November 2-6; and Okinawa: November 9-13. He entitled his lecture series "The Christian Life." In every retreat Maston lectured for eight or nine sessions.

Maston preached in worship services at base Protestant chapels. On the last Sunday of October, he spoke in two morning services for the Eighth Army chapel in South Korea. In November on the first Sunday, again it was for tandem services at the army chapel in Zama, Japan. For the rest of the itinerary, Maston preached once each at the army chapel in Okinawa and at the air force chapel in Yokote, Japan.

On his arrival at Eighth Army Headquarters in Korea, the chaplain told Maston something that caused him some apprehension. The chaplain said there would be some special guests attending the eleven o'clock service on the following morning. Syngman Rhee, the first president of the Republic of Korea, and his wife had indicated their intention to be present. General Carter B. Magruder and his wife would accompany the first couple. The general was commander of both the United States Army and the United Nations Armed Forces in Korea.

The prospect of preaching before such dignitaries made Maston reconsider his sermon. His prepared message centered on the present reality of eternal life. The truth derives from 1 John 5:13, "That ye may know that ye have eternal life." He had told the chaplain's office in advance the subject of the sermon. Briefly, Maston entertained the notion of changing the sermon because of the guests. He recalled the words of a brigadier general cautioning Maston to avoid any reference to Japan. "Syngman Rhee hates Japan," emphasized the officer. Wisely, the professor decided to proceed with the original message as planned.

At the second morning service, the special guests were seated toward the front on the right-hand side. When the service reached the time for the sermon, Maston felt a surge of added strength as he stood at the pulpit. The message flowed with confidence. The preacher frequently eyed the president. With eyes fixed on the preacher, Syngman Rhee listened intently. Manifest interest spurred on the speaker in the pulpit. The sermon had a telling effect.

After the benediction, Maston descended the platform moving toward the presidential party. The chaplain introduced him to President and Mrs. Rhee and General and Mrs. Magruder. Syngman Rhee grasped Maston's arm and pulled him closer, whispering an unforgettable comment into the professor's ear. "I wish I could live up to everything you said this morning," offered the president. It was a poignant moment.

The sermon in the Eighth Army Headquarters' chapel on that Sunday morning by an unordained professor was a milestone. It had been a long, long journey from his first forgettable preaching effort thirty-eight years before in the Smithwood Baptist Church. On that occasion, Lucy

Cooper had tried to console him with kind words. If only she could have been in that service when he stirred the heart of a president!

Maston's military hosts thoughtfully provided ample opportunities to break away from the demanding lecture schedule. They gave him a guided tour of Seoul. One afternoon they furnished a helicopter and pilot to take him on a tour over some of the Korean theater of war. They flew over the Demilitarized Zone created by the United Nations truce. Near Panmunjom he saw the Freedom Bridge over which repatriated prisoners were transported during the prisoner exchange.

Swooping to another area, the pilot pointed out a particular house on the North Korean side. He explained that it was the building that housed the twenty-three American defectors who refused repatriation. Only one named Dickinson finally elected to rejoin his countrymen in the South. Below the hovering craft, Maston saw clearly the "bridge-of-no-return" over which that lone soldier walked.

When the helicopter returned to its base and landed the pilot heaved a sigh of relief. "I'll tell ya, Perfesser," he told Maston, "every time I go over the DMZ I get the shakes. Sure am glad to get back on our side."

"Thanks for tellin' me now, Fellah," said the older man with a smile. In flight the pilot had showed no signs of uneasiness. Maston did not know to be nervous. The tour held him in constant fascination. He was too busy scanning the terrain to sense fear.

Maston demonstrated his knack for rapid rapport with

persons anywhere in the world. He entered military culture with a ready heart and mind. Servicemen and officers alike responded with alacrity. An immediate fellow-feeling resulted. Never would he compromise his convictions or his conduct to suit the situation. This earned him widespread respect.

Many military men are notorious for their drinking and smoking. It pleased Maston that during the entire tour in the Orient, he was never once offered either an alcoholic beverage or a cigarette. It saddened him to observe some chaplains who had no such scruples. However, the military men with whom he associated did not regard him as a prude. They perceived in him a good sport.

Early in the tour in Korea he was the guest of honor at the commanding officer's mess on a Saturday night. He sat next to the CO at the head table. Sitting strictly by rank, there were five brigadier generals and several colonels also at the table. In spite of military protocol there prevailed a warm feeling of camaraderie.

When waiters brought cocktails they served Maston lemonade in a cocktail glass. One of the chaplains sneaked up behind him and plopped a bright red maraschino cherry in the lemonade, making it look like a cocktail. Maston responded good-naturedly by joining in the spontaneous laughter. It reminded him of seminary students making fun of him at the annual faculty takeoffs. He felt complimented that the military men had accepted him so readily.

The lecture series started off well in Korea. Maston based his teaching on the accumulated resources of his classroom notes from Southwestern Seminary. "I talked to them the same as if they were Baptists," he explains.

During one of the sessions when there was a break, Maston went out of the building to stroll around the grounds of the retreat center. Two of the chaplains asked if they might join him. He gladly consented. They were both of the Lutheran persuasion. It impressed him as they talked that these were men of solid convictions. In jest they granted that if Maston would only change in one or two points they would welcome him into the Lutheran Church. That brought on a round of chuckles.

Later at the beginning of the session that followed, Maston told the group what his walking companions had said. One chaplain at the back of the room blurted out, "Why, we'd take you like you are!"

Another voice spoke out, "He must be a Methodist!"

Maston confides. "And sure enough, he was!"

Typhoon Emma afforded Maston the opportunity for intimate fellowship with one chaplain, Edward Mize. The violent storm swept over Okinawa, canceling the lectures for a day and a half. On a Thursday morning, it was "Condition One" for the typhoon. The chaplain invited Maston to "ride it out" in his home. Mrs. Mize was away on a journey. The invitation furnished the professor with a breather and a chance to relax.

It was some relaxation!

The storm whipped up strong winds that buffeted the house. The two men went outside around the house to close the window shutters. After nightfall, torrential rains dumped ten inches in three-hours' time. After the rain, winds up to 125 miles an hour assaulted the island. The chaplain stayed up through the night. Maston slept fitfully at best.

At 2:15 AM a violent gust of wind struck the side of the house on which Maston was sleeping. That woke him up for good. He helped Chaplain Mize mop water as it streamed under the front door and at windows that had no shutters. They collected several tubs of water. By morning, Emma had moved on to a point a hundred miles east. At noon someone gave the all-clear signal. The sessions resumed in the evening.

Maston's opportunities for fellowship were not limited to military personnel. The schedule provided free time on Saturday mornings and Sunday afternoons and evenings. Maston used the time to contact missionaries and to visit some of the Baptist work. In the area of Seoul, Korea, he renewed friendship with his old friends John and Jewell Abernathy. At the same time, he spent time with former students Don and Juanita Jones.

Maston spoke in Baptist churches in all three countries on the itinerary. Usually, it was for a Sunday evening service. In Tokyo, he attended the dedication of a new building for the Baptist church. There were a dozen or more of his former students present. He stayed with the Dub Jacksons.

On Okinawa, there were at the time no Southern Baptist missionaries. However, Maston met an American Baptist missionary, Ed Bollinger. The work he had begun impressed Maston. There were Southern Baptist military personnel and their families active in the Central Baptist

Church. It brought great satisfaction to Maston to see in every place the fruits of missionary diligence.

At the conclusion of the whirlwind tour, the unanimous verdict declared it an outstanding success. Letters came bringing military salutes. The chief of chaplains, Major General Tobey, who had sent Maston on the assignment was very complimentary.

> Your contribution to the chaplains was particularly vital and strengthening for them. Their report . . . expresses gratitude for your effective spiritual assistance. They also expressed in glowing terms your personal contribution in private conversations.

Chaplain R. C. Hohenstein, US Navy, wrote:

> Yours was a most difficult task—to present a theological subject to groups with such widely different backgrounds. . . . I, for one, was thrilled to find such general and genuine acceptance of the material which you presented in such a winsome and evangelical manner. In this art you are both Maston and a master!

A Southern Baptist chaplain exclaimed in his letter of appreciation, "You certainly won a lot of friends for Southern Baptists."

Perhaps the most moving word of appreciation came from Chaplain Albert Shoemaker, a Lutheran. He suggested, "In addition to being our teacher, you were our friend and fellow, all of the Chaplains in Korea felt that you had done something real 'special' for us."

Upon his return to Texas, Maston wrote to Chaplain

Wallace Hale. He referred to the lecture tour as "one of the richest [experiences] of my life." In the press, he reported that he was profoundly touched by the masses in the Orient. He said:

> I can never get away from the impact of the market places in Naha [Japan], Okinawa, and particularly in Seoul, Korea. I thought of the words concerning Jesus that He had compassion on the multitudes. And I kept repeating to myself, *These people were created in the image of God. These are people for whom Christ died.*

With emphasis, Maston expressed his newly found conviction, "I do not believe here in the United States that we realize the tremendous missionary potential men in the military have. Not just the chaplains, but all the military men." On his second long journey, Maston, servant-pilgrim, had discovered fresh vistas of missionary service.

3

And Miles to Go

The servant-pilgrim approached one of life's momentous crossroads in the fall of 1962. He met an obstacle and chose a direction perceived to be within God's will. It opened up many new avenues of service, enabling him to pursue a pathway of service that made a career out of retirement.

God's Will

Maston faced the possibility of voluntary retirement at the age of sixty-five. Love for teaching made him reluctant to retire. Nevertheless, there were competing interests. It was a crucial decision.

In addition to his professorial responsibilities, two exigencies laid claim to Maston's time and energy. In the first place, he sensed the urgent need to be more of a help to Mommie with Tom Mac. The care of their adult invalid was not getting any easier as they both grew older. In the second place, yet another interest demanded attention. Maston's penchant for writing goaded him to increased output. As an active professor, he had produced nine books. Most of the writing dealt with significant contemporary issues. He had already established himself as a popular author.

Accordingly, Maston proposed to the administration of Southwestern Seminary that he continue teaching with some decrease in responsibilities. Along with the two concerns he particularly wanted to devote more time to the graduate program in ethics. Specifically, he requested a reduction of his classroom-teaching load.

With a counterproposal the administration effectively rejected Maston's request. The matter of establishing bad precedent became a paramount concern. He received the choice of standard alternatives. If he wanted, he could retire at the end of the current academic year. Otherwise, he could continue but with the course load required of all faculty. There could be no exception. It was a classic nonchoice, an offer he could not accept.

Maston requested retirement, and the trustees of the school accepted. With feeling he wrote to Gene, "I have a deep conviction that this was the best thing for me to do ..." However, he confessed to a twinge of anxiety, "I must honestly say that there are some things about it that I dread quite a bit." His main regret was the distance retirement would put between himself and students. It was for him the most telling loss of all.

The seminary also experienced a loss. Not only did it lose an outstanding professor, but it missed having him during five very productive years. A former colleague and lifelong friend, Frank Means, expressed the view of most of Maston's admirers. "I have always felt the seminary made a fundamental mistake in 'allowing' him to retire when it did," said Means.

During Maston's last semester of teaching, he impressed students with his usual positive attitude. One former student recalls, "He took the disappointment of retiring earlier than he wanted with grace and poise. . . . There was neither bitterness nor rancor."

Regarding Maston's retirement, close friend and colleague, Jack MacGorman, said it well, "For every *no* God has a better *yes.*" It was the yes that "made all the difference." The changed direction leading from the crossroads opened new horizons in the will of God for T. B. Maston.

The pursuit of God's will has consumed Maston's entire lifetime. His formula for decision making is simple and direct. In private prayer, he seeks divine guidance. He explains further,

> My policy through the years was that many times I needed to close my prayer by saying to the Father, "Now Father, this is what I think You want me to do. If I'm making a mistake, give me additional light, or in some way stop me.' Then I've found that as I start to take a step, he does give me a sense of direction.

Frank Means reflects on Maston's compelling search, "He—more than almost anyone I have ever known—seeks earnestly and diligently to know the Lord's will. Then he gives himself wholeheartedly to doing it."

In classroom notes kept for posterity, one reads familiar maxims in Maston's own handwriting. They epitomize the man's pursuit:

God's will should be our supreme concern. . . . It is better to suffer and be within the will of God than to be free from suffering and yet be outside his will. . . . We need to be sincere when we pray, "Thy will be done," for God may just do it. . . . Follow your heart and not your head.

William Pinson, executive director of the Baptist General Convention of Texas, is another former student and a former ethics colleague of Maston. "A key in his ethic," insists Pinson, "was . . . the will of God." It is also the keystone to Maston's missionary vision. For Maston, missions is a preeminent consideration in the doing of God's will. It has been a strong element in Maston's role as counselor and no less important in his own involvement in missionary endeavor.

Maston's most popular book is *God's Will and Your Life*. The publication appeared a year following his retirement. The publisher has sold more than seventy-two thousand copies. They released a new edition twenty-four years later.

In his book Maston insists that it is possible for persons to prevent the accomplishment of divine will. The thought informs his theology of the will of God. It affirms the God-given freedom of human will. Yet human freedom expresses itself best within the very will of God. Maston indicates that this is a paradox.

However, there are times when the fulfillment of God's will depends on the cooperation of others. A third party can thwart the doing of God's ideal purpose. In this respect Maston readily acknowledges that the primary person could be the one mistaken. At times one does misread the will of God for oneself. Nevertheless, others may fail to cooperate and, therefore, frustrate God's will.

The writings of Leslie D. Weatherhead have influenced Maston considerably. Weatherhead discerned three distinct aspects in understanding the will of God. They follow a progression: there is the ideal or intentional, the circumstantial, and the ultimate will of God.

Maston sees in the circumstantial will of God a rationale for understanding how others can hinder the accomplishment of God's ideal purpose. He bases his thinking on certain experiences in his own life. One is from a time in the 1930s when Maston was a young professor. It was when he had the strong impression that the Lord wanted him to join the staff of the Southern Baptist Foreign Mission Board. However, Maddry, executive secretary of the Board, passed over him in choosing someone else. In utter sincerity Maston surmised that someone had bypassed God's will. Maston reached three conclusions,

1. It is possible for individuals, agencies, or institutions to come between us and the will of God.
2. When we are willing to do our Father's will and through no fault of ours it does not work out, He will care for our interests. . .
3. We can also be sure that God has a will for us in the new circumstances we face in life.

Jesse Fletcher, president of Hardin-Simmons Baptist University who also studied under Maston, holds the professor and his writing in high esteem. During the time that Maston was writing his book, Fletcher was personnel secretary of the Foreign Mission Board. They sometimes conferred about missionary candidates on the seminary's campus. In reading the preliminary manuscript of Maston's book, Fletcher questioned the validity of Maston's conclusions. He suggested they could lead to

> hasty judgments about the will of God: (1), adjust ourselves to what we judge to be a thwarting factor; (2), seek a secondary will . . . (3), and totally miss . . . a far more intricate pattern concerning God's will . . . as providential.

More recently Fletcher has commented, "The dynamic dimension of God's will precludes any secondary will."

The two men are probably closer together on this point than their words show. Fletcher focuses more toward Christian vocation in his assessment of Maston's idea. On the other hand, Maston's attention comprehends also the dynamics of life's other significant decisions. To be sure, for him, such considerations include the Christian's calling.

Terse sayings continued to flow forth from Maston's wisdom. In the classroom he often said, "Life is too short to do anything other than the will of God." When the Christian's safety was in question, he would offer, "The place of duty is the place of safety . . . the will of God is always best."

Maston is a veritable Southern Baptist guru of God's will. Throughout his long career, he has been in demand to speak on the subject on campuses around the United States. Once again in the Student Missions Conference at

Southwestern Seminary on March 7, 1987, he led a session on "Discovering God's Will for Your Life."

Maston's character and life embodied what he taught about the will of God. Regardless of how he may have interpreted the circumstances surrounding his retirement, one thing is clear. He faced the future with consistent determination to "prove what is that good, and acceptable, and perfect, will of God" (Rom. 12:2*b*).

Retirement from the Southwestern faculty never meant retirement from seeking and doing God's will. For Maston, retirement truly meant a new beginning. It was a different journey in the larger quest of sovereign will. His determination has been relentless.

Jack MacGorman expounds on Maston's obsession for God's will, such as the time of Maston's massive heart attack in 1979. The doctors did not expect him to survive. MacGorman visited him in the hospital. Seminary colleagues had cautioned that MacGorman should only spend two or three minutes in the patient's room. He fully intended to honor the caution. He did not sit down. He spoke only briefly and then offered to leave. In spite of this Maston alertly insisted that MacGorman remain longer.

Maston had been doing some profound thinking. He said,

> When I came to the hospital I made Mommie promise that she would not pray that I would come home [get well] but that God's will be done. If I'm able to recover I must know the will of God for it.

He continued by expressing concerns regarding certain

trends in Southern Baptist life. It burdened Maston that upward mobility to the upper middle class was bringing about a resultant desertion of the grassroots. In a hospital bed while recovering from a near-fatal heart attack Maston's heart and mind focused on his beloved denomination. Was there anything he could do to help?

MacGorman summarizes:

> The upshot of it is that there was a man who couldn't even conceive of an extension of his life without God's will being the primary consideration—"If life extends I must know why." . . . He wouldn't let me go for a long time, and he was doing most of the talking! This epitomizes the man for me. I've since read in published articles concerns that he expressed to me that day. The man simply can't think of living without harnessing it to the will of God. This is the constancy of his life.

This is the constancy that after retirement led Maston on toward new adventures in missions.

Other Journeys

Like a medieval troubadour, T. B. Maston has ventured to many fields fulfilling his love affair with missions. The old-world troubadour fared forth from one princely domain to the next singing of courtly love. Maston journeyed to the far reaches of God's kingdom serving those who declare the good news among the people. His travels have carried him to latitudes and longitudes ranging from the exotic to the prosaic.

Maston's missionary globe-trotting stretches over more

than forty years. Passage into missions began while he was an active professor. It could not wait for the favorable opportunity that retirement affords. Nevertheless, his eventual departure from the Southwestern faculty released him more fully for extensive traveling.

The itinerary reads like an astronaut's diary in slow motion.

Mexico:	Prior 1954—three one-week speaking engagements
Latin America:	Summer 1954—eight-week circuit of eight countries
Orient:	Fall 1959—four-week series of US military chaplains' retreats: Korea, Japan, and Okinawa
Mexico:	July 1961—one-week mission meeting
South America:	May-June 1963—All Brazil Missions Conference, and Central Field Conference, Columbia
Latin America:	February-March 1964—North Field Conference, Mexico; and South Field Conference, Chile
USA:	June 1964—Foreign Missions Conference, Glorieta, New Mexico
USA:	June-July 1965—Foreign Missions Consultation, Miami Beach, Florida
Middle East:	March-July 1966—accompanied by Mommie and Tom Mac—fourteen-week tour of Lebanon, Jordan, and Israel, returning via Europe
South America:	July-August 1967—the Maston trio:

	eight-week itinerary including visits and assignments to eight countries
Hawaii:	February 1968—the Maston trio: two speaking engagements
USA:	September-October 1968—Chaplain's seminars: Norfolk, Virginia, Pensacola, Florida
Mexico and Central America:	July 1970—three countries for mission meetings
USA:	1970—El Paso, Texas, Spanish Baptist Publishing House: missionary prayer retreat—one of several such engagements
Bermuda:	1973—speaking engagements
Bahamas:	1975-1976—two trips in back-to-back years for speaking engagements

There are two more journeys that do not appear in the chronology. Maston suggests he made a total of seven trips to Mexico. This means there is one more visit south of the border with no date indicated. The occasion was either a mission meeting or youth retreat. Likewise, the date is missing for his participation in a chaplains' seminar for the Materiel Command in Alexandria, Virginia. It probably occurred in the early to mid-1970s. Colorful vignettes emerge from his peregrinations. Maston's unassuming geniality charmed everyone he met. Missionary Charles Campbell went from Argentina to the South Field Conference in Chile in 1964. He traveled with Maston after the conference for visits to some of the Baptist work in Chile. Campbell found Maston's style refreshingly different from the usual visitor. Campbell considered that Maston avoided manifesting the condescending manner typical of many denominational executives. Instead he showed great empathy for the missionary in his situation. Campbell calls him another Barnabas, "the great encourager."

Maston identified readily with the local people. In Latin America friends and close acquaintances customarily greet with the *abrazo*. Missionaries from North America soon learn how to share the open-hearted embrace. It signals a positive measure of acceptance when nationals make the first move to embrace.

In Vina del Mar, Chile, Maston and Campbell participated in a service at the Baptist Church. Maston preached while the missionary provided interpretation. Judging by facial expressions among the congregation it was clear the message had inspired the worshipers.

The pastor also responded with profound feeling. At the conclusion of the service he approached Maston opening his arms for an embrace. With ready affection Maston hugged the pastor enthusiastically. Campbell marvelled at how easily and naturally it had happened. Maston showed no inhibition whatsoever. He took to the *abrazo* like a bona fide South American national.

Maston visited Charles and Martha Bryan a second time in Colombia. Mommie and Tom Mac accompanied him on his eight-week excursion in 1967. The Bryans' second child, Elizabeth, was two years old. Once again

Maston became the surrogate grandfather in the Bryan household. On this occasion he had some competition for her affection.

Tom Mac charmed Elizabeth from the very beginning. She responded merrily to his smiling countenance. She hugged and kissed him without hesitation. Her ready acceptance of him developed naturally. He delighted in her company. Often when they pushed him from one room to another she would ride on the foot pedals of his wheelchair. Tom Mac wore his exuberant smile as the pair glided through the house.

One day the Mastons lingered at the table after a meal. Charles had rushed off to an appointment. There was time to talk. Martha Bryan unloaded to Maston and Mommie about her serious problem as a missionary homemaker. Her role as a missionary working with the local Baptist congregation competed with her home responsibilities. She loved the people in the church but she also felt a deep devotion toward her immediate loved ones in the home.

Martha's family needed her sorely. Charles followed a full schedule of missionary activity every day. He needed her support as an efficient manager in household matters and as a companion and counselor in his work. Both fourteen-year-old Carol and two-year-old Elizabeth demanded time and energy. Each had her own particular claim for motherly attention. Martha was torn anxiously between her church and her home.

Maston listened intently to her problem. When Martha finished confiding her problem, she concluded with a sigh saying, "I just don't know what to do! How can I be a good

wife and mother and serve the Lord at the same time?"
There was a pleading in her tone of voice.

With a low voice and a twinkle in his eye, Maston
measured his words. "Well, Martha," he said, "it seems
to me you have the same problem that many pastor's
wives have in America too. My suggestion to you is that
while your children are small and growing, you should try
to make an *A* in family life and a *B* in church work. Then
later when they are grown and don't need you as much,
try for an *A* in church work and a *B* in family life!"

It was so wonderfully clear. Martha smiled as his words
touched her heart. "That's the answer I need!" she exclaimed. She has carried his counsel throughout her career.

The Mission in Colombia provided the Maston trio with
a furnished apartment at the Cali seminary for several
weeks. It gave them a base for Maston to meet engagements in the surrounding countries. The arrangement was
a more relaxing situation for Mommie as she looked after
Tom Mac's daily needs.

On one occasion when Maston was participating in
meetings in neighboring Ecuador, a mild earth tremor
struck the area. It was very early in the morning. Maston
sat straight up in bed. The rumbling sound and the quiver-
ing movements induced novel sensations within. He wondered if Mommie and Tom Mac were experiencing the
same one simultaneously.

In the apartment in Cali, Mommie had doubly locked
the door before going to bed that night. At 5 AM she
suddenly awakened with a strange throbbing within. She

sensed a quick spell of dizziness. She thought to herself, *It's a heart attack.* She worried that if anything happened to her, the missionaries would have a difficult time getting in because of the locked door. It concerned her because of Tom Mac's helplessness.

Half awake, Mommie felt calm again. In an instant it started again. This time her eyes were open enough to see pictures swinging on the walls. The bed was trembling. The quaking of the earth penetrated her awareness. Although it lasted only two or three minutes, she felt it was longer. It certainly was long enough! As soon as it stopped she got out of bed and checked on Tom Mac. He was soundly asleep.

Later the same day she and Tom Mac went out on the seminary campus for a stroll. While she was rolling Tom Mac along, she met missionary Ben Welmaker. He greeted her asking, "How did you like our sample earth tremor?

She replied, "Well, it was enough of the real thing for me!"

Tom Mac proved his ability to move from place to place and to adjust readily to new situations. In Sao Paulo, Brazil, the Mastons stayed with the Thurmon Bryants. On a few occasions both Maston and Mommie would leave Tom Mac for brief periods of time. Tom Mac contented himself to remain with some friend or acquaintance. He enjoyed it better when there was something for him to watch. He took pleasure in gazing out a window to watch people pass by. Television also appealed to him.

One day when the senior Mastons were gone, Thurmon Bryant remained with Tom Mac. Thurmon placed the younger Maston in the living room in front of the television. When he turned the set on a US rerun of "Gunsmoke" appeared on the screen. Satisfied that Tom Mac would occupy himself happily, Thurmon busied himself in another part of the house with personal matters.

Once when Thurmon walked through the living room he observed that Tom Mac was laughing in his characteristic shrill manner. The missionary paused to see what caused his laughter. The scene showed Marshall Matt Dillon talking to Kitty. Of course, the Brazilian producers had dubbed the film in Portuguese. Suddenly Thurmon understood the humor that brought on Tom Mac's laughter. No doubt Tom Mac had already seen the show back in the States. It amused him to hear Mat Dillon speaking Portuguese instead of English.

The Mastons stayed in the Bryant home for several days. The Bryants have four sons. The first two are adopted. Some years later they received two more sons by natural birth. When the family sat around the table with the Mastons as guests, it was a sizable gathering. The mealtime conversation was usually very jovial.

On one such occasion, Maston had observed five-year-old David eating heartily. Maston asked Thurmon, "Is it true that you missionaries are given a raise in salary after you have another child? Is that the way you get a raise?

Thurmon answered, "That's correct."

Maston continued, "Watching this boy eat I think you came out on the short end of the stick!"

Maston's personable ways won the hearts of many wherever he traveled. Justice Anderson explains why:

He had a knack, sort of what we call the missionary gift, of being able to be interested in other people. If they began talking about him, he would change it to them by saying, "What about you?" You really felt that he was personally interested.

His various journeys furnished Maston with abundant opportunities for him to exercise well beyond retirement his gift for teaching. He is the inveterate teacher. He is a consistently inspiring teacher and speaker. It is this quality that gained for him more invitations than he could accept.

After Maston had spoken at the Mexican Mission's annual meeting in 1970, he received a letter from missionary Jimmy Hartfield. In gratitude Hartfield expressed the sentiment of all of the missionaries. He wrote, "Your messages were just what we needed to reawaken our love one for the other, and to point us toward a life of greater service for Christ."

Maston did more than inspire his hearers. He also motivated them with his prophetic call for ethical concerns. These were no less imperative for missionaries than for Christian leaders in his homeland. Bob Adams, missionary to Argentina, described Maston's ringing appeal for thoroughly Christian social concern:

His call was to a responsible, personal renewal of faith in Jesus as the Christ, that would inevitably manifest itself in better relationships with fellow Christians, and would consequently leaven the Latin society for good and toward justice.

His counsels for missionaries and nationals alike were sage. When he spoke to the Brazil Missions Conference in 1963, Maston spoke plainly about the realities confronting the missionaries:

> I think you know that you are not down here as a protagonist of American culture. You are not down here to defend political democracy, as much as we believe in it. No, the people of Brazil are going to have to find their own political structures; . . . to work out their own economic problems; and I am quite sure when they get the work done, that it will not be exactly what we have in the United States.

Alan Neely relates an interchange between Maston and the missionaries on an issue that was very much alike at the time. The question probed his counsel regarding the rising Peasant Leagues. It was a Brazilian movement that represented the masses and their many grievances. Maston countered with the question, "Are some of your Baptist people in them?"

The answer came, "The president of the Peasant League Movement in Paraiba is also the leader of one of the Baptist churches in that state."

Maston then responded:

> In that case, my viewpoint is that you should not discourage them. . . . If the program of these Peasant Leagues contains legitimate desires of the peasant class of the country, then I think the more of the Christian influence you give them, the better it will be.

In an article Maston wrote after his return from Brazil following the conference he drew some emphatic conclusions. He acknowledged that the missionaries in Latin America were facing hard decisions. He cautioned, "They must not be maneuvered by the Communists into a position of opposition to the masses and seemingly become defenders of the privileged."

In 1964 the Southern Baptist Foreign Mission Board invited Maston to present an address at the annual Foreign Missions Conference in Glorieta, New Mexico. The title assigned to him was, "World Issues Confronting the Missionaries." In preparing for the assignment, Maston could not rely on his own preconceived notions. His keen sense of responsible research would not allow it.

He wrote to two dozen or more missionaries around the world to ask for their input. "Pass on to me what you consider to be some of the major issues that you face . . . political, economic and social." He wanted to discover if there was a consensus among the missionaries. He also wanted "to check my own thinking to see how nearly I am correct." The missionaries honored his request with a strong level of response.

Similarly, Maston traveled to Miami Beach, Florida, in the summer of 1965 to deliver a background paper for the Foreign Missions Consultation. He entitled it: "This Revolutionary World." The parameters for his address were the whirling changes in the world's political, social, and economic arenas during the previous decade. He probed to discern the consequences of such developments for the Christian movement in general and the foreign missions endeavor in particular.

At the end of his presentation, Maston gave a succinct thirteen-point summary. There follows immediately "A Personal Conclusion." He gave a sobering and incisive appraisal of the contemporary situation facing the missionary of the sixties. Its relevance and validity still hold.

The reader will understand better Maston's profound and prophetic insights from a quotation of the first paragraph of the conclusion:

> We regret to have to say that we do not believe that the rather anemic, pallid type of religion found in most of our churches and in most of our individual lives is adequate for the kind of world in which we live. This means, among other things, that if the missionary is to meet the challenges that face him, he must not simply transport to the mission field the type of Christianity found, in the main, in our churches. He must get a personally fresh grip on the vitalities of the Christian faith. This faith must become in him the dynamite of God. He must remain open and responsive to the leadership of the divine Spirit, recognizing that the Spirit may lead in previously untrodden paths.

Explosive faith, "the dynamite of God," motivates not only missionaries but also Christian leaders of every role and function. Maston gained this insight early in his missionary invovlements. For one thing he perceived that various kinds of chaplaincy ministries represented a legitimate category of missions. His experience was mostly with the military chaplaincy. Its missionary character had already proved itself to him.

Maston's reputation as an effective trainer of chaplains lingered long after the Orient retreats. It left a durable impression in the minds of the chaplaincy leadership. Once again, nine years after the Oriental Pilgrimage, the chaplains called him to serve.

Rear Admiral James W. Kelly, chief of chaplains of the Navy, invited Maston to conduct training courses for four weeks in the fall of 1968. The invitation called for two weeks in Norfolk, Virginia, in September and another two weeks in Pensacola, Florida, in October. Mommie and Tom Mac joined Maston for the second week in Pensacola. He considered it a missionary venture even though it didn't carry him outside of the United States.

Kelly requested that the courses center on the theme, "Contemporary Ethics and the Christian Faith." He would treat in particular crucial problems confronting the navy chaplain of the day. The real admiral identified the problems as "marital and premarital sex; family planning and abortion; war; justice and love; problems of vocation; management/command relationships, and leisure time.

Each training course required eighteen hours of lecturing per week. In advance of the sessions Maston requested that he might do his lecturing from a seated position. Commenting that "the most mature part of me are my knees," he suggested that teaching from a seated position would conserve his energy.

The lectures scored a success again at both of the bases.

The chaplains acclaimed Maston's teaching. Their letters applauded him for his effective and inspiring leadership.

Sometime in the early seventies the Headquarters' Chaplaincy office of the United States Materiel Command summoned Maston to participate in a special seminar. They asked him to share in the session with scholars from the Roman Catholic and Jewish faiths on current ethical issues. He represented the Protestant perspective. The challenge of this opportunity was different from the previous experiences. It prodded Maston to make exceptional preparation. It called for thorough scholarship in his chosen field. It also blended with his penchant for the missionary situation.

Maston's journeys after retirement describe a specialized career in missions. He was a volunteer in the sense that he performed most of his work without remuneration. It was truly a labor of love.

His frequent companion on several of his journeys to Latin America was Frank Means, the area secretary for the continent. Their friendship went back to the years that they were colleagues together at Southwestern. Although they did not always travel together, their paths often crossed at some meeting of missionaries.

In 1967 the two men participated in a conference of missionaries in the Central Field. During one of the sessions Charles Bryan, the field representative for the Central Field, made a special presentation to Means. It was a twenty-year pin awarded by the Foreign Mission Board in recognition of service longevity.

When it was Maston's turn to speak on the program, he

began by jesting in a kindly way about the presentation. "I hear that you gave a pin to Frank Means for twenty years of service with the Foreign Mission Board. He's pretty lucky." He teased, "Here I served Southern Baptists for forty-one years at Southwestern Seminary, and I haven't gotten a thing for it."

The following day at the first session Bryan called Maston to the front. With straight face and solemn voice he said, "Today we want to honor you in recognition of your forty-one years of service to Southern Baptists as a professor at Southwestern Seminary." At a signal, another missionary produced a bright red streamer. It was a yard long. On it they had marked every one of the forty-one years. Bryan pinned it on his chest. It hung down below his knees.

The group exploded into hilarious laughter. Maston joined in the merriment wholeheartedly. How thoroughly he enjoyed the missionaries because they have such a ready sense of humor. Once again the troubadour was in his element!

Missionary-troubadour, T. B. Maston, sometimes reverted to his old role of professor. On one of his journeys he was more the professor. Mommie and Tom Mac were the troubadours.

Mission to Beirut

"Mommie," Maston called as he entered the back door and moved toward the kitchen. She wasn't in the kitchen. He turned right and marched into the family room. There he saw her busily sewing. "I've got a letter in my hand from the Foreign Mission Board," he blurted out. "They want me to go to the seminary in Beirut next year and teach!"

Isn't that where Finlay and Julia Graham teach?" she asked. "I'd dearly love to go to that part of the world."

"I wouldn't think of going without you," he vowed. "But what about Tom Mac? If we took him along, it would be a big undertaking. I don't know if he could manage it," explored Maston.

"He does pretty well riding in the car in long trips. It wouldn't be too much different," Mommie observed.

Maston wondered aloud, "I don't suppose Gene would be able to come and take care of him. Do you think so, Mommie?"

"For how long will it be?" she inquired.

"Well, they want me for the entire spring semester. That's sixteen weeks. However, I've got too much work to do on my manuscript before I can go. It's my idea to offer to teach for a half semester. That'll be two months," he informed her.

"Gene's work wouldn't let him be away for as long as that," she observed.

"Do you really think we could take Tom Mac?" he probed.

"I'm game. Let's try it!" said Mommie emphatically.

Her words dissolved his indecision. Mommie always showed remarkable spunk. Now her Southern Appalachian backbone asserted itself. She relished the challenge. Moreover, she had wanted to go to the Middle East for as long as she could remember. Such a golden opportunity must not pass unanswered. That was the resolve that spurred him to agree. They would go as a family. It would be their first journey together!

A month later Maston responded to a letter from Finlay Graham. In his letter to Graham he said, "I still have some misgivings about us attempting that long trip with Tom Mac." However, he went on to assure his friend that he would inquire about preliminary details such as passports, visas, and airline schedules. Then they would finalize the decision.

When the time came, the original determination to go remained firm. The Mastons were undaunted. They pursued plans for the journey accordingly.

Nineteen sixty-six was the year of the Mastons' Middle East pilgrimage. They departed at the end of March. The itinerary included three countries: Jordan, Israel, and Lebanon. First, they visited the Baptist Hospital at Ajloun, Jordan, in early April. Their hosts were Dr. and Mrs. August Lovegren. Next they went to Haifa, Israel, where they visited the Dwight Bakers.

By mid-April, they reached Beirut, Lebanon. They remained there for the next two months while Maston fulfilled his teaching assignment at the Baptist Seminary. After the seminary's commencement, they traveled overland through Damascus to Jerusalem. Their week-long visit in Jerusalem enabled them to visit many of the biblical sites in the area.

En route to the United States they stopped briefly in Switzerland to visit the International Baptist Seminary at Ruschlikon. The three-and-a-half-month odyssey ended

in mid-July. It was the longest time span for any of Maston's journeys.

Upon arriving in Texas, the Mastons immediately realized the trip had been a success! The long and exhausting
itinerary had gone without a serious problem. Tom Mac
had proven that he was a seasoned traveler. Now they
knew they could travel as a family unit. It opened the door
for other trips.

There was only one contrary incident for Tom Mac
during the entire journey. It occurred when they deplaned
at Beirut. Two airlines attendants took him in the chair
down the steps from the aircraft in a very awkward fashion. They carried Tom Mac backwards with his head
down. The sensation of this unusual position alarmed him.
It was greatly upsetting for the forty-year-old invalid.

His parents rushed to reassure him and help him regain
composure. They soothed him back to his usual calm
manner. A group of missionaries and Lebanese Baptists
were present at the airport to greet them. They had observed the episode and the manner in which the elder
Mastons had handled it—so tenderly and so skillfully. It
left an indelible impression on all. Through alertness and
loving care, the Maston pair had remedied what started
out to be an unfortunate scene.

Missionary Jim Ragland expressed the consensus of all
whom the Maston family touched during their tour. He
wrote, "The fact that he wanted to come with his wife and
invalid son, with all that this meant in terms of hardship
and adjustment, is a powerful expression of his love for all
men."

Jack MacGorman taught for a year at the Arab Baptist Seminary on the heels of the Mastons' tour. "Wherever Maston goes," MacGorman declares, "there are lingering echoes." He suggests, "They took Tom Mac into the Arab world where the Tom Macs are hidden." Again he remarks, "By their example of willingly bringing Tom Mac out into the open, they gave a non-verbal witness to the Arabs."

An unexpected role for Tom Mac developed as the journey progressed. He drew the spotlight from the beginning. It remained fixed on him throughout the tour. He upstaged his father. For once he became the star!

There was no chagrin or sense of rivalry. Maston and Mommie took pleasure in the attention Tom Mac was receiving. His enjoyment of it pleased them. So many showered Tom Mac with kindness and love. That is how they wanted it.

During the visit to Israel they were the guests of missionaries Dwight and Emma Baker in Haifa. Their third-story apartment on the slopes of Mount Carmel furnished a panoramic view of the harbor.

From Haifa the Mastons visited scenes in biblical Palestine. Every morning Bron and Bill, the Bakers' teenage sons, carried Tom Mac in his wheelchair down three flights of stairs—fifty steps—to the street level. After a day of touring when Mastons returned in the evening, the boys carried him up again to the apartment.

They visited many places associated with the life of Jesus. At each site either Maston or Mommie would carefully explain its significance to Tom Mac. They would say,

"Jesus lived in this town." Or, "In this place Jesus performed a miracle." Or, "Here is where He healed a blind man." Tom Mac would always respond with the smile from ear to ear that has become his trademark.

Baker recalls, "His pleasure seemed to be the source of theirs and mine! It was remarkable how well he held up, never seeming to get tired of the sight-seeing."

Nancie Wingo, missionary to Lebanon, recounts a time when they motored in the mountains to view the famous cedars of Lebanon. She stopped at a filling station for refueling. The station attendant observed Tom Mac and because very curious. Speaking in Arabic he asked Nancie what was wrong with the handicapped one. She explained that he was born with the condition and had carried it throughout his life.

Maston asked Nancie about their conversation. Upon learning about the man's curiosity, Maston asked Nancie to interpret something that he wanted to say. "Tell him," he urged, "that people should not be put away just because they are retarded. [Pause for interpretation] They deserve to be treated like the human beings they are. [Pause] That's why we like to bring our son out in public."

Tom Mac was the center of attraction everywhere. In Damascus his presence created a major sensation. They pulled up in front of a hotel to eat lunch in the dining room. Immediately, local people swarmed around the car gaping at Tom Mac. There were children and adults pressing against the car. The crowd was so thick there was not room enough to get Tom Mac out and into the wheelchair.

Immediately, an elderly man came to the rescue. Wielding a walking stick and scolding loudly in Arabic he drove the crowd back. Soon there was enough space to install Tom Mac in the wheelchair and to move into the hotel.

At one biblical site, the guide was a priest of an Eastern Christian church. The presence of Tom Mac on the tour so distracted him that he could scarcely direct the tour. It was such a bizarre novelty for the guide that he forgot his speech. He asked them repeatedly. "Where did he come from? . . . How did he get here?"

One Sunday, a missionary arranged for Maston to speak in a church in the mountains near Sidon, Lebanon. The missionary stressed that Mommie and Tom Mac should also come along. After the service, the pastor of the church invited the Mastons and the missionary to lunch in his home.

At the table, the Mastons sat in their usual formation. Tom Mac sat between his parents with Maston to his right. Maston, as always, fed Tom Mac. The Pastor and his wife observed thoughtfully. Occasionally, during the meal indistinguishable sounds drifted upward from the basement. It puzzled the Mastons.

On their return to Beirut, they asked about the strange sounds. The missionary disclosed the pastor's secret. It was the pastor's twelve-year-old retarded daughter! The parents confined her to the basement. Furthermore, they had a retarded adolescent son whom they had committed to an institution.

Suddenly, Maston understood what had happened. The missionary had schemed to get the Mastons into the pastor's home. He wanted Maston to demonstrate firsthand a more Christian way to care for the handicapped.

It is certain that Maston's loving care for his son inspired students far more eloquently than any of his lectures. Fawaz Ameish, pastor of the Amman Baptist Church in the capital of Jordan, cherishes an experience he gained during the Maston pilgrimage. Fawaz shared the incident with missionary Emmett Barnes, president of the Arab Baptist Seminary. The Jordanian pastor delivered the keynote message at the twenty-fifth anniversary of the founding of the seminary in June, 1986. Fawaz had been in the first graduating class of the seminary.

He told Barnes that he, Fawaz, had returned to Beirut in 1966 during Maston's teaching assignment at the seminary. Since there were Jordanian students graduating, the pastor came for the commencement activities. The occasion gave Fawaz the opportunity to meet Maston and to observe him in action. He affirmed, "People were as influenced by the way Dr. Maston dealt with his son as by what he taught."

At the banquet for graduates, Fawaz accompanied a senior student from Jordan, Samir Sweiz. Samir had worked closely with the Mastons during their stay at the seminary. In the home he had often helped them in caring for Tom Mac. At the table, the two Jordanians sat opposite the Mastons.

Fawaz watched entranced as Maston fed Tom Mac in his customary manner. The pastor perceived the love and tenderness that Maston transmitted toward his helpless son in the performance of such a commonplace act. Fawaz thought of all of the years the father had been doing this for his son. His emotions stirred within. Tears began streaming down his face as he leaned toward Samir. He whispered, "This is a very heavy and not an easy cross."

Samir counseled, "Don't say 'cross,' because Dr. Maston says this is not a cross. This is a duty God permits us to fulfill. The cross is something else. Dr. Maston has taught us that it is when we accept voluntarily to obey the Lord, follow the Lord, and serve in spite of the cross."

Fawaz told Barnes, "It was a great lesson. I had a new understanding."

The learning of lessons was a mutually shared experience. The Mastons gained much knowledge and understanding, too. This was especially true for Mommie. Arab culture ignited her interest. There was much to learn.

In Jordan the Mastons attended the Sunday service in the Ajloun Baptist Church. It is the custom for men and women to sit separately on opposite sides. Mommie sat with Alta Lee Lovegren. At the close of the service after the pastor pronounced the benediction, Mommie heard "Amen." She started to move out of her seat toward the exit door. Alta Lee caught her by the arm and whispered, "Wait."

Mommie replied in a low voice, "Why? Isn't it over?"

Alta Lee confided, "The women can't leave until the men go out first."

"Well, who do they think they are?" Mommie whispered back to her companion. Indeed, she had much to learn!

Some of the learning experiences came serendipitously.

One day August Lovegren took the Mastons and a friend with three children on a drive through the Jordanian countryside. They picnicked in a beautiful olive grove. It was a balmy spring day.

As the party continued the drive, they soon saw an enormous black tent set off from the highway a few hundred feet. Lovegren explained that it was a Bedouin encampment. The Bedouins prefer to use black goatskins as material for tents. Maston expressed his desire to take a picture. Lovegren suggested that it would probably be all right, but it would be well to ask permission first.

Mommie stayed with Tom Mac while the rest went to the tent to inquire. She waited a long time before Maston returned to the car. He informed her that the Bedouin hosts insisted on serving tea to the visitors. Since it was a distance across rugged terrain, there wasn't any way the wheelchair could negotiate cross country. Maston offered to stay in the car with Tom Mac while she went to the tea party. Mommie consented with obvious excitement mounting within her.

The long tent was divided into two sections. The partition resembled burlap. The hosts placed sleeping mats for the guests to sit on. Mommie thrilled to see an infant wrapped in swaddling clothes—narrow cloth strips wrapped around the child's body and limbs. The Bedouins say that it helps their arms and legs to grow straight. The Bedouin women passed the baby around for everyone to hold. Mommie saw that he was "a happy little fellow."

She observed smoke rising to the top of the tent on the other side of the partition. Soon two women came from behind the partition into the visitor's side. One carried a long tray with small glasses. The other brought a full pot of tea. Mommie asked Dr. Lovegren if it would be safe to drink. He assured her that since they had boiled the water to make the tea it would be safe. The Bedouin poured tea into each glass for his guests.

Mommie put the glass to her lips and sipped a drop of tea. Her taste buds registered: *SWEET!* It was sickening sweet. She managed to get most of it down. The women also served some flat cookies. They were quite edible. The host offered everyone a second cup of tea. Mommie declined but was careful to emphasize her gratitude for the kindness.

Bedouin hospitality overwhelmed her. The host was exceedingly cordial and gracious. He invited them all to stay for supper. He offered to get a young lamb from the flock that grazed nearby. He would have it slaughtered and roasted. Then they would serve it with some Arab bread and more tea. Lovegren gracefully excused his party. He informed the host that Mrs. Lovegren was expecting them in Ajloun for the evening meal. Mommie recalls, "I was kind of glad we didn't accept the invitation!" One must take the learning of culture in stages. She wasn't ready for the full meal yet.

The Mastons adjusted well to their temporary environment. They had learned to love the people in every place. Even Tom Mac had attached himself to certain persons. The cook and the seminary's driver had become his favorites.

Mommie reveled in the exotic flowers that grow in the

Middle East. One day on the campus of the Beirut seminary, she visited with one of the missionary wives, Maxine King. Mommie noticed as she was leaving the house that the gardener was working in the flower beds. She spied a local variety of iris. They are a bright red and have smaller blossoms than the American flower. Maxine offered her some iris to keep. Mommie gladly accepted. She put them in a tin can with fresh soil. They soon took root.

When time came for the Mastons to leave Lebanon, Mommie determined to taken some of the Middle East back to Texas. She wrapped the iris and some geranium cuttings in wet paper toweling and put them in a plastic bag. For part of the return journey she carried them in her carryon. On the last flight across the Atlantic she slipped the flowers into the pocket of Maston's topcoat without his knowledge.

They passed customs smoothly. It relieved Mommie there had been no question or awkwardness about the flowers. Maston didn't know to be relieved. Later when she retrieved them from his coat pocket, she had to explain about the flowers. It startled Maston to learn that he had brought contraband flowers into the United States!

Mommie planted the cuttings in the yard at home. The iris survived. They graced her garden for several years. The geraniums didn't make it.

Maston returned to cultivate in a different kind of garden. Foreign Mission Board staff responsible for training missionaries called on Maston for help. It was one of his postretirement activities that evolved in the mid-sixties.

The servant-pilgrim became a gardener of new missionaries.

Equipper of Missionaries

Like a vehicle in constant service, Maston made a turnaround within two weeks and struck out for Virginia. There was scarecely time for rest and recuperation from the exhausting tour of the Middle East. The retirement calendar was unremitting in its claims on his time and energy.

Maston flew to Bristol, Virginia, for a week of training with a special group of Baptist young adults. In 1964, the Foreign Mission Board had inaugurated a two-year program of missionary service for college graduates under twenty-six years of age. The following year the first selected group underwent an intensive six-week training. The campus of Virginia Intermont College provided facilities for it. Maston had participated in the initial training during the week of July 5 - 10, 1965.

He went again the second year. The journeyman of the First group had rated him highly for a return performance. Maston went to share some of the fresh insights furnished by the recent Middle East experience. His clear design was to give them wise guidance and encouragement. He relished the chance to relate to young men and women with such a lofty sense of purpose.

Maston imparted to the young adults his conviction about the role of a missionary journeyman overseas. He based it on his careful observations of effective missionaries serving in many places. He contended, ". . . . if they did a better job of representing Christ, . . . the evangelistic results would be greater, if there were more consistency of life."

Remembering his first feeble effort at preaching in the Smithwood church, the words of Lucy Cooper stuck indellibly in his awareness. In his counsels to journeyman he relayed her words of wisdom, " . . . the greatest sermon you'll ever preach is the life you live."

Maston impressed upon the young adults a model of servanthood. It was not an affectation. Instead, it flowed out from his authentic personhood. Leo Waldrop, missionary to Surnam, participated as a journeyman in the 1966 journeyman training. He recalls a very ordinary experience that illustrates Maston's unstudied service to others.

Maston's week with the journeymen came at the end of the training period. At the close of the week, the journeymen gathered on the steps of a campus building for a group picture. Several journeymen stood with cameras in front of the larger group. Each wanted to take a photograph with his own camera. Maston sensed a need. Immediately, he stepped out of the formation and volunteered to be the photographer.

It was like a Norman Rockwell painting. Maston stood facing the group. The journeymen were poised on the steps hamming it up as they tried to strike suitable poses. There were twenty cameras lined at Maston's feet on the sidewalk. Methodically he clicked away one by one with every single camera.

As Maston did his work, Waldrop took his own mental

picture of the scene. It remains vivid in his memory album. The subtitle under Waldrop's imaginary photo reads, "This man is quick to serve."

There is a vast difference, however, between servanthood and servility. Maston illustrates the distinction. It's the difference between true meekness and a wishy-washy abject spirit. A college English professor once gave an apt definition of meekness. He described it as "a fair steed under control."

During the first journeyman training session in 1965 there were two young men who constantly tormented the visiting leaders with pointed questions. They grew increasingly obnoxious as the weeks progressed. Sitting together in the back of the group, frequently they would interrupt the lecturers with their barbed queries. They showed no more respect for Maston.

After they had needled him several times with impudent questions, the annoyance became unbearable. An exasperated Maston stopped his lecture. He singled out the disruptive hecklers and addressed them directly.

> You fellows are trying to put me in a corner and embarrass me. No teacher likes that. I did not have to come here. I came here because I thought the Lord wanted me to do so. I came to try to share, as best I could, some things that may be of help to you folks who go out around the world as journeymen.

The room settled into a tense silence. The two did not respond. Undaunted, Maston proceeded with the lecture. His words squelched the troublemakers.

Maston wondered if his words had come across too harshly. Perhaps he had put his continuing role in the journeymen program into jeopardy.

At the close of the lecture several journeymen came to him. They said, "Dr. Maston, we love you and we're sorry for what those two have been doing to you. We're glad that you put those two in their places."

Later Maston went to Louis Cobbs, director of the journeyman program, and W.L. Howard, director of that year's training program. Maston reported what had happened. Their reaction surprised him. As one man they concurred, "That's the best thing that has happened this summer! Those guys have had it coming to them for a long time."

Summer after summer, the invitations came for Maston to share in journeyman training. He became the "Old Faithful" of the annual sessions. Eventually, the training sessions transferred to the campus of Meredith College in Raleigh, N.C.

Early in the program the Board elected Stan Nelson as director. He, too, was strongly in favor of having Maston participate. Once he wrote, "You have been a large influence on my life. I will feel very cheated if you cannot share with the young people this summer."

In accepting Maston replied.

Let me express my appreciation to you for the invitation. I know these invitations cannot keep on coming indefinitely, but as long as I am able to go and the invitation comes,

I am going to accept the opportunities I have to be with young people.

Nelson confides one reason for wanting Maston on a regular basis. He considered the venerable professor to be an reliable litmus test for proving the suitability of journeymen for overseas service. Nelson observed how the individual journeyman responded to Maston. It became an accurate indication of the journeyman's potential. Nelson comments, "Young adults that respected this man were those I believed would fit into other cultures."

Notably, Maston regarded the journeymen as deserving of his continuing interest after they went to their fields of service. He maintained a correspondence with those who stayed in touch with him. It was the same with journeymen as it was with career missionaries.

Jimmy Maroney went as a journeyman to Ghana in 1967. He taught in the Kumasi Academy. When the news broke in 1968 of the assassination of Martin Luther King, six-to-seven-hundred students came to Maroney's back door. They expressed shock at the news and wanted to learn the details. He tried to satisfy their concerns and to console them by expressing his own deep sorrow. Soon the crowd dispersed.

Maroney described the incident in his next newsletter. He made a personal assessment of King's career and the impact of his assassination on Ghanaians. He included a quotation from the *Ghanaian Times.*

Maston received the newsletter and responded promptly. He commented to Maroney, "You've joined the ranks of those trying to bring reconciliation between black and white." Two years later Maroney met Maston on the campus of Southwestern Seminary. Maroney referred to the interchange of letters about Martin Luther King. A tear formed in Maston's eye as he said of King, "That's one man who needed to live."

Maston's capacity for pathos distinguishes him. It reflects his manifest concern for the downtrodden and the poverty-stricken masses. He communicated well the burden of Christian responsibility to journeymen. It may explain in part why he was the perennial favorite.

Between 1965 and 1984 Maston served in all but four of the annual journeyman training sessions. In 1969 a commitment to teach at Golden Gate Baptist Seminary prevented him from participating. On three other occasions he missed because of illness.

The summer following a massive heart attack in 1979, Maston's first engagement was with the journeymen. He went again in 1981. Alan Neely portrays a typical scene from Maston's last week with them. Maston was giving a devotional message when Neely joined in the session. Neely quietly took his seat at the back. He describes the impressions garnered from what he saw and heard.

> I was just astounded that here were all these young people sitting—listening— it seemed to me with great respect and interest. He was just as casual and matter-of-fact . . . but it was prepared . . . and he was just as lucid as can be.

The journeymen watched him, too. They tried to digest all that he fed them. It was a veritable feast. A journeyman once expressed in verse the impact felt by his group under the influence of the "old man." David Gooch wrote:

In these days
We have watched you
We have seen
A man
Who walks with God
Responsibly as He demands.
And we pray
That when we reach
"Maturity" we will have walked
Along the cutting edge of life
As you, old man.

Maston reflects on his experiences with the journeyman program with warmhearted gratitude. His memory of serving in the career missionary orientation, likewise, stirs up favorable emotions. Regarding both endeavors he affirms, "These engagements . . . meant as much to me in a real sense of fulfillment as anything I've ever done."

In 1967 his role as an equipper of missionaries expanded to include career missionaries of the Foreign Mission Board. It was the year that the Board developed a more comprehensive missionary orientation program than in previous years. David Lockard was the new director. He invited Maston for the first orientation session at Ridgecrest, North Carolina. It was for the week of October 16-21.

For the next seventeen years Maston participated annually in the training event. After the program transferred to Callaway Gardens in Georgia, he sometimes went twice a year. He canceled in 1978 and again in 1979 because of illness. However, he returned to the 1980 session after his heart attack.

For the second orientation in 1968, Mommie and Tom Mac accompanied him. They traveled by road. Since Tom Mac was already a proven traveler, it was a feasible journey. Encouraged by the experience the family came regularly with him to the fall sessions.

Usually, Lockard scheduled it so that the Mastons would be at the conference for Tom Mac's birthday. The staff planned on annual birthday celebration. It was a poignant experience for new missionaries as the Mastons modeled family life with a handicapped son.

From the beginning Lockard suggested two specific assignments. One task for Maston was to provide a series of inspirational Bible studies each morning. The second approach was to offer a cluster of lecture-discussions on applied Christianity in the afternoon sessions. The two assignments became the regular Maston agenda for the subsequent years.

The request for the devotional Bible studies surprised Maston. Although he established his ethical teachings firmly on scriptural principles, biblical studies were not per se his primary field. Lockard's suggestion challenged Maston to dig hard in preparation for the Bible studies.

Lockard's confidence in his ability to produce such a series pleased Maston very much. The assignment pointed him in a new direction that expanded his fruitfulness and influence. It resulted in a popular series that excelled in originality and inspiration.

Maston developed his themes under an umbrella topic: "Little Words with Big Meanings." He focused on biblical words such as: *love, faith, walk, compassion,* and *touch.* He also motivated the new missionaries with his stress on the will of God and servanthood.

The Bible studies he has given from year to year provide the substance for several of Maston's books. He has woven some of the material into various works. Furthermore, Maston based two titled specifically on the material presented to missionaries. One is *Real Life in Christ;* another is *Words of Wisdom.*

The series on practical Christianity dealt with what Lockard terms "the horizontal dimensions of the missionary life." Maston's topics describe the scope of his material: "The World from Which You Go," "The World to Which You Go," "Race Relations," Ethical Decisions of the Missionary," and "The Missionary and the Will of God."

Maston stimulated his listeners to realize the practical implications of servanthood for missionaries. "Whatever you are going to do," he insisted, "you are going there to minister to the needs of people." He warned, "Don't get any ideas of superiority because the Lord has called you to be a missionary." He urged, "The highest service we can render is that which springs from within with no thought of reward."

Universal testimony from colleagues, friends, and missionaries all points to one outstanding aspect of Maston's teaching. It is something that was true of his professional years as well as his postretirement ministries. He *lived* what he taught. He consistently fulfilled Lucy Cooper's definition of the "best sermon."

Lockard relates the anecdote of one of Maston's rare encounters with a law-enforcement officer. Late one night, Maston was driving his car to Callaway Gardens near Pine Mountain, Georgia. It was a narrow, winding road. Being deep in thought, he frequently veered over the center stripe. There was little traffic.

One car approached Maston from the rear. Immediately, when Maston saw flashing lights in the rear view mirror, he knew it was the state highway patrol. He pulled the car to the shoulder and waited for the officer to come. He realized that it was probably the result of his wandering over the center line. Chagrin settled over him as he sat quietly in the car.

The patrolman came to Maston's door. Maston rolled down the window. The man wanted to see his driver's license. As Maston handed it to the officer, he calmly introduced himself, "I'm T. H. B. Maston. I'm on my way to Callaway Gardens."

The officer said firmly, "Do you realize that your car has been weaving back and forth on the highway?"

"Yes sir, I know that," said Maston.

The patrolman looked at the license. "Are you from Texas?" he enquired.

"Yes, I live in Forth Worth," the older man replied.

The officer began to sense that he did not have a drunk on his hands. He began to feel uncomfortable. He lowered his tone of voice and reduced the volume. "Are you with the Baptists at Callaway Gardens?" he asked.

Maston replied, "Yes, I am here this week to lead in the training program for missionaries."

"Oh, I see. Well, I'm very sorry to have stopped you, Mr. Maston. I thought maybe you were intoxicated," explained the patrolman.

Maston laughed. "I can honestly say that I have never taken a drink in all my life."

The situation relaxed. A smile formed as the officer said, "I believe you and I'm sorry for the delay."

"Oh, no," replied Maston, "you were right to stop me. I certainly was weaving across the center line, and there's no excuse for that. I can see why you may've thought that I was under the influence of alcohol. You were only doing your job."

"Thank you for the way you've taken this. I don't stop very many who are as pleasant as you," remarked the patrolman.

Maston asked, "Sir, would you mind giving me your name? I would like to write to the State Highway Department and commend you for being so alert and for doing your duty with such courtesy and consideration.

The patrolman gave Maston his name and identification number. The exchange concluded. Maston started the car and proceeded on his way. He kept the car on the right side of the center line all the way to Callaway Gardens! The next day he wrote the promised letter of commendation.

Maston has a genius for defusing a potentially tense

situation. His poise, quiet grace, soft voice, and directness all work together to relieve the tension.

Wendall Parker, missionary to Guatemala, recounts an episode at the 1967 orientation at Ridgecrest. The topic for the day was "Race Relations." There was a young black woman in the orientation group. The Foreign Mission Board had appointed her to be its first black missionary.

During the time for open discussion, the group felt greatly inhibited. Some who wanted to ask questions or make comments were reluctant to speak out. Most of the new missionaries had already learned to respect and appreciate the young woman. They held back for fear of inadvertently saying something wrong. They didn't want to offend or slight her in any way.

Maston quickly sized up the situation. He summoned the young lady to come to the front. He asked her to frankly share her personal feelings about racial differences. She readily expressed herself with tactful grace. Her insights and confident manner allayed the tension. It soon encouraged the group to open up. Together they pursued a fruitful discussion.

A large measure of Maston's effectiveness issues from what Keith Parks calls, "the authenticity of who he is." He is transparent and single-hearted. His amiable manner dissolves pretense. He gives himself to others freely, and he receives freely. That is literally true.

Once in Lockard's office at Callaway Gardens Maston admired his friend's necktie. Lockard said, "Well, if you like it so well, then I'll just give it to you." He loosened the tie and removed it from around his neck.

It nonplussed Maston at first. He said, "Oh no, Dave, I didn't mean for you to do that! I was just saying, 'It's a pretty tie.'"

Lockard insisted, "Listen, Dr. Maston, I want you to have it." He firmly placed it into Maston's hand. "Now it's yours."

With a broad smile Maston drawled, "Well, if you put it that way, Okay, I'll take it. Thank you, my friend. I assure you I'll wear it."

Lockard attests that the next morning at breakfast, the gentleman was sporting his hand-me-down tie. Furthermore, Lockard recalls that he saw the tie on Maston frequently during subsequent years at Callaway Gardens.

Another prosaic experience illustrates Maston's upretentious manner. It occurred during the 1970 orientation session with Jimmy Maroney. Upon completion of his journeyman service Maroney and his wife, Kay, had pursued career missions. Once again they associated with the esteemed professor.

It was such a commonplace thing, but for some reason, it was memorable for Maroney. It was also typical of Maston's naturalness.

The Maroneys were sitting together with Maston, Mommie, and Tom Mac at the table in the dining hall at Callaway Gardens at the evening meal. Maston had emerged from the cafeteria line with corn bread and a glass of milk on his tray in addition to the main course. In customary fashion he fed his son and alternately ate from his own plate. As soon as he could, he crumbled the corn bread into the milk as surreptitiously as possible. Maroney and Kay watched in warmhearted amusement. They recognized Maston's East Tennessee culture coming through. It was so wonderfully human.

It was this man who so ably trained missionaries for a decade and a half. In the fall of 1985, the Missionary Learning Department of the Foreign Mission Board gave Maston a plaque. It acknowledges his role as an equipper of missionaries. I was visiting in the Maston home on the day that Maston received it in the mail.

It reads:

> Dr. T. B. MASTON
> IN DEEP APPRECIATION
> FOR MANY YEARS IN
> HELPING TRAIN
> MISSIONARIES
> JOURNEYMAN

When I handed it back to Maston, Mommie was standing nearby. She said to her husband, "I suppose you're going to put it in the drawer with the rest of the plaques. Aren't you?"—laughter—The point was clear. Maston is not one to display his laurels.

The servant-pilgrim had traveled many miles. Many journeys composed his pilgrimage. He reached the time when traveling tapered off. The creeping years restrict. He would remain close to home.

Maston's pilgrimage reminds one of the prophet Isaiah's utterance,

He giveth power to the faint; and to them that have no
might he increaseth strength. Even the youths shall faint
and be weary, and the young men shall utterly fall: But
they that wait upon the Lord shall renew their strength;
they shall mount up with wings as eagles; they shall run
and not be weary; and they shall walk and not faint
(40:29-31)

With regard to Maston one is tempted to add, "and he
shall sit and not quit." There were several unfinished bits
of business before he could sleep.

4
Before I Sleep

"Jesus and Mommie are the two folks closest to me." Maston confided this once to a group at the Missionary Orientation Conference in Georgia. To say such a thing appears contrary to the explicit word of Jesus about the priority of discipleship over family. One remembers Jesus insisting, "If any man come to me, and hate not his father, and mother, and *Wife*" (Luke 14:26, author's italics). It is a vexing statement.

Surely, the Lord is not advocating hatred of any sort. It must be hyperbole. The believer's love for Christ should be so great that any human love pales by comparison. Mark well, Maston's love for Christ is preeminent.

The paradox of linking Mommie and Jesus compares favorably with Jesus' own paradox. From the cross in sovereign tenderness, Jesus looked down on His earthly mother and His beloved John. He bonded them together with His words, "Behold thy son!" . . . thy mother! (John 19:26-27). Christ cared for her! He bequeathed to her the legacy of a close human relationship. Certainly, such human bonds give pleasure to God.

Devotion: Family and Missions

Maston's missionary pilgrimage was a shared odyssey. Even when he traveled alone, his family entered vicariously into his journeys. His devotion to his family and to missions was mutually inclusive. They interweave in the fabric of his life as a servant-pilgrim.

The aftermath of a second close encounter with death underscores the intertwining relationship. It shows the interaction of Christian commitment and family devotion. It was the reprise of his first near approach to death forty-six years before. In 1933 it was pneumonia.

On October 27, 1979, Maston experienced a mild heart attack. Mommie rushed him to Harris Hospital in Fort Worth. While he was still in the intensive-care unit, he suffered a second, more severe coronary occlusion. It damages 25 percent of his heart. Fortunately, he was in the right place to receive instant maximum care.

Once again Maston survived. Soon the crisis passed. One day Dr. Osborne, his attending physician, came into Maston's room to inform him of the favorable prognosis.

Maston asked the doctor, "How much more time do you say I have to live?"

Osborne replied, "Long enough for you to do all you want to do." He knew his patient well.

Maston thought of all that he wanted to accomplish. He needed a definite answer. "You may not know what I have in mind to do yet." he remarked. "How many years would you say?"

"About three years," said the physician cautiously.

Later when Mommie came to visit, Maston shared with her the doctor's good report. She said, "I'd say it'll take you at least ten years for you to finish what you've already started on." She looked at him directly and asked. "Now what are you going to try to get done?"

Seven-plus years later, Maston had published many articles, three books, republished a title, and produced privately a short monograph about Mommie. In addition, he returned to journeyman training and career missionary orientation several times. He continues to assert, "As long as the good Lord leaves me here, I ought to be busy about something."

Maston's first agenda after returning home from the hospital concerned a matter that he considered long overdue. His prompt response to Mommie's question, "Now what . . . ?" was to write a thirteen-page booklet introducing her to his wide circle of friends.

He delights in describing the situation for writing it. Unsuspecting, Mommie often sat with him in the sitting room while he was writing about her. Because she respects his privacy, she never looks over his shoulder or pries into his papers.

Maston's tribute flows forth in glowing terms, "She is the hero of this family." He tells her story as it intermingles with his. Their courtship and marriage established the basis for their remarkably long relationship. In June of 1986 they observed their sixty-fifth wedding anniversary.

Maston carefully delineates what a help she has been to him. He points out that she is not only strong physically but also emotionally. As a green-thumbed lover of flowers, she buries "a lot of self-pity in her flower bends." While he was in graduate studies at Yale, she coached him in French and German. Once when he was recuperating from a stomach ulcer, the doctor prescribed goat's milk. They bought a goat, and Mommie milked it for years to provide for his need.

Mommie has taught Sunday School since she was sixteen years old. The only lapses occurred during her college years and during Tom Mac's adolescence. Since 1969, she has taught a class of ladies seventy years of age and older. Most of them exceed eighty. Maston attests that she is very thorough in her preparation from week to week.

Maston and Mommie have effectively translated their early missionary commitment into a lifetime of service to missions. They support missions in their church. They have traveled to mission fields. He has trained missionaries. He corresponds extensively with missionaries. And together they pray consistently for missions.

Glen Edwards, a former pastor, discloses something Maston once told him in conversation. The professor informed his pastor that sometimes when he has insomnia, he prays for missionaries. He calls them by name, "looking into their faces through his mind's eye, and recalling to memory the places where they serve."

In 1978 I was a missionary in Africa. I received a form letter from my former professor. Maston informed me that he, Mommie, and Tom Mac follow the prayer calendar regularly. He wrote, "We breathe a prayer for you on your birthday." It was a heartening word.

Gene Maston affirms that such active praying for missions was a long-standing practice in the Maston household. Breakfast is the customary time for their family devotions. It is the time for Bible reading and prayer. Gene says, "I cannot remember when we did not pray for missionaries./ He stresses that it was not a vague or general "God bless all the missionaries."

Instead, Maston will read the names of missionaries whose birthday occurs on that day. Then they try to recall some characteristic or circumstance about each person they know personally. Sometimes they may reminisce about an experience or a place involving the missionary. There is a missions map of the world on the east wall of the breakfast nook. It shows the places where Southern Baptists are serving. Frequently, Maston will point out a particular country. If the country's name is difficult to pronounce, they will look it up on the map. They often mention a specific need for prayer.

Tom Mac is very much aware of the discussion and prayer time. Gene recounts one morning when his father called the name of a missionary to Colombia. They remembered his from the time when they stayed at the seminary in Cali. Somehow they associated the missionary with the earth tremor that occurred while they were there. Tom Mac responded with a broad smile and an audible squeal that is his way of laughing. They all had a good laugh about it.

Maston's devotional focus on missions explains his affinity toward missionaries. They exert a kind of magnetic pull on him. It is the same attraction that lured him to visit them in their places of service. At the annual meetings of the Southern Baptist Convention, Maston was sure to attend the regular reception for missionaries.

Mrs. Wanda Pippin recollects such a reception during the 1978 meeting in Atlanta. Maston's presence signaled to her encouragement: "I love you and I believe in what you are doing. I stand back of you with my interest and prayers."

Maston not only expressed his affinity for missionaries by seeking their fellowship but also through correspondence. An avid, tireless letter writer, he has accumulated voluminous files of letters over a long career. The list of his correspondents is formidable in both quality and quantity.

He gave a gentle reprimand to Gene in his letter of May 14, 1962. A previous unanswered letter provided the stimulus. With a fatherly hint Maston maintained, " . . . I have always made it a practice to answer my mail. Most of it gets answered quite promptly."

The unanimous consent of missionaries supports his contention. He has a flawless track record in faithful response to letters received. "You could never write him a letter that he didn't answer—no matter how busy he was," claims James Crane, retired missionary to Mexico.

Dwight Baker, retired missionary to Israel and India, concurs, "Dr. Maston has over the years . . . answered every one of our printed newsletters, whether we added a personal note or not." Baker describes the content of his letters, as "News of his family, a sketch of his wide range of activities, and expressions of concern and interest in the work of the Lord where we serve."

Through correspondence, active fellowship with missionaries, faithful praying, and involvement in the local church, the Mastons thoroughly participate in missions. Their devotion to missions is wrapped up in their devotion to one another as family. The remarkable influence that Maston has in missions is not merely the impact of one man. It is the influence of a family unreservedly committed to missions.

Influence Through Servanthood

Servanthood permeates the life and ministry of T. B. Maston. He, himself, embodies a fusion of the will of God and servanthood. "It is God's will that I serve." This is the recurring theme of his pilgrimage. The servant-pilgrim inspires many who intersect his life's orbit with the genuineness of his servanthood. This is particularly true of missionaries.

Charles Campbell, missionary to Argentina, represents well the missionary consensus:

> The reason most missionaries are ready to listen to him is . . . his willingness to serve anywhere and do anything the Lord may desire. . . . He is not out trying to impress someone and is not a denominational climber. He is my ideal (best so far) of one who is truly a servant of the Lord.

Journeymen were not exempt from Maston's exhortation to serve. Kevin Peacock, a former journeyman to Scotland, was in the last journeyman training session that Maston attended in 1984. The ex-journeyman enrolled at

Southwestern Baptist Seminary after completing his service in 1986.

One day in the seminary library, Peacock participated in a very commonplace episode with Maston. It is memorable because it demonstrates simply and eloquently the man's innate sense of serving.

Peacock was leaving the men's rest room on the third floor of the library just as Maston entered. The two exchanged cordial greetings. Rumpled paper towels lay scattered on the floor. Maston commented, "It's too bad when people miss the waste container and leave these on the floor." He used his cane to push the paper into a pile. Then he stooped down to pick up the paper. Considering Maston's history of heart trouble, that was a risky thing for him to do.

Peacock felt slightly embarrassed. He hoped the older man didn't think he was one of those who had missed the waste can. It chagrined Peacock to think that he had been unmindful of the paper. Quickly, he helped pick up the remaining trash to spare Maston further bending over. The older gentleman thanked him. Peacock mused as he walked away, *What a moving lesson in servanthood that was!*

When one considers the enormous influence of T. B. Maston, there comes a temptation to overdo the adulation. Thoughtful admirers will resist the inclination to confer on him an unwanted sainthood. Maston, himself, suggests that certain long-standing friends express their regard for him too generously. He considers them incapable of objectivity.

Regarding commendations, Maston prefers the short-and-sweet variety. A reference letter used for his first trip to Latin America in 1954 provides an example. The letterhead shows, "Scott Bros. Grain Co., Inc., Fort Worth, Texas." The double-spaced text reads:

> TO WHOM IT MAY CONCERN: This is to certify that we have known the bearer, Dr. T. B. Maston, for about thirty years. We are pleased to say that he is a Christian gentleman above reproach, of unimpeachable character, honorable in all transactions, possesses unusually high intellectual qualifications, and is absolutely loyal to the country in which he lives.

The signatures reveal the Scott brothers: "C. W. Scott, Pres.," and "R. L. Scott, Vice Pres." Two illegible stamps from Latin American consultates appear on the letter.

Notwithstanding Maston's desire to the contrary, many tributes accumulate. The temptation to lionize him is too irresistible. Charles E. Myers was among the first of Maston's graduate students. The two have had a lifelong friendship carried on mostly through correspondence. Myers praises Maston as one having had "more influence in the lives of those who have shaped our denomination in the past forty years than any other man." He continues by stressing, "Apart from my family, he has influenced me more than any person I have ever met. He also is the best man I have ever known."

The admiration of another long-standing friend includes the objectivity of a historian. William Estep, distinguished professor of church history at Southwestern Seminary, expressed considerable esteem. He wrote:

> So from my experience with Dr. Maston as a [his former] student, as a fellow church member, as a colleague on the faculty at the seminary, and from my reading of his many books, I consider him one of the truly great Christians I have ever been privileged to know, and my life has been the richer because of it.

"The glory of a teacher," observes Maston, "is that he can have former students who do many things that he never could do." Referring to his own former students, he continues, "There are a good many of them on the foreign mission field."

He considers the prolonged and intense struggle over missions with which he and Essie Mae wrestled a necessary preparation. Through the tortuous experience God was getting Maston ready for the missionary influence he would later exert on his students. It also trained him to be available for the various missionary journeys.

Mommie reveals her side of the experience. Her desires to serve overseas in missions was probably more tenacious than Maston's. She offers, "At first, I was disappointed but as time went on we adjusted to it." She further suggests that Maston "had a sense of being a different kind of missionary."

Undeniably, his involvement in missions developed along unconventional lines. Maston proliferated his missionary zeal through a long line of students who went overseas. Miss Ray Buster, a close friend from their student years in the seminary, suggested the idea to him on his first journey. She concluded:

> Well, I can understand now why the Lord kept you there [in Fort Worth]. . . . If you'd have come out here, you'd have been in one place. There you're touchin' folks that are goin' around the world!

Dwight Baker gives a most discerning appraisal of Maston's influence. Baker emphasizes Maston's

> unique ability and gift to sharpen other men and women to the point of their greatest effectiveness. He is not a missionary nor does he claim to be [in the usual sense], but he produces great missionaries. A whet-stone doesn't cut, but it produces sharp knives that do.

Maston was ever alert to encourage those committed to missions who experienced obstacles. Dudley Phifer, missionary to Malawi, tells of his pilgrimage with his wife in missions. Initially, the Foreign Mission Board indicated certain hindrances that would keep them from appointment. It discouraged the Phifers considerably. They wrote a form letter informing their friends about the apparent rejection by the Board. Maston was on their mailing list.

Maston replied with strong personal encouragement that they not give up on seeking foreign mission service. He urged them to prove their sense of missionary calling. Once they felt certain of it, they should patiently wait for a period and then reapply to the Foreign Mission Board. Maston mentioned that he knew of several candidates who had successfully done this.

The Phifers received other responses with similar counsel. Resolutely they perserved. A few years later they reapplied. On the second time around, their candidacy succeeded. At last the Board did appoint them to their chosen field in Africa.

Maston not only stood behind those who succeeded, but he also helped those who failed missionary appointment. He provided an emotional anchorage for rejected candidates.

Yates Bingham illustrates this point. Bingham pursued ministry in the pastorate and eventually in the U.S. Air Force chaplaincy.

Maston's compassionate understanding and counsel supported Bingham through a series of experiences. The professor shepherded his student through seminary studies and eventual ordination to the gospel ministry. When the Binghams faltered in their pursuit of missionary appointment, Maston was the ever-ready cushion in the trauma of rejection.

He successfully encouraged Bingham to do graduate studies. Soon after returning to the seminary, a serious illness struck Bingham. The Professor made several pastoral-like visits to manifest concern for his student. It typifies so well Maston's personal care for his students. Bingham says "The main thing . . . is that I knew he was *always* there."

The servant-pilgrim extended his influence beyond the wide sphere of former students. He touched the lives of many during his extensive travels. With students, his influence worked on them over an extended period of time.

During Maston's journeys, however, he impacted persons over much shorter periods of time.

One whom he affected deeply is Chaplain Rodger Hill. Following Maston's seminars in Pensacola, Florida, in 1968 Hill wrote:

> During my life time I have met very few persons who, by the power of their personhood and integrity, have significantly influenced me as a person. With all honesty I can confess you are one of those few, and I know that I am a better person for having known you—even for all too short a time.

The remarkable aspect of Maston's influence on Hill is that it penetrated immediately. It needed only a short reaction time.

Maston's lengthening shadow falls on second-generation missionaries, too. Missionary children whose parents studied under Maston often give evidence of his influence. Kent Parks grew up in a missionary home in Indonesia. He is preparing for missionary service. His parents, Keith and Helen Jean, were former students of Maston. Today, Keith Parks is the competent pilot at the helm of the Foreign Mission Board.

Kent was unaware of Maston's silent influence in the home, but he reveals:

> I cut my teeth on Maston's ethics while I was growing up in Indonesia. My mom and dad had thoroughly imbided in it. However, I did not realize it until I came here to study his works in seminary. Then I knew where they both had received their ethical outlook.

Stan is the youngest son of the Parkses. Like his brother, he, too, wants to serve as a missionary. He gained an unforgettable impression of Maston during a chance visit. He was a college senior at the time. Stan's mother, Helen Jean, agreed to substitute for the ailing Maston at a Student Missions Conference on the Southwestern Seminary campus. She accepted his assigned topic: "Discovering God's Will for Your Life."

Helen Jean wanted to receive firsthand input from the esteemed professor in preparation for her sessions. Stan went along out of curiosity. He had heard so much about Dr. Maston. At last he would meet him.

They entered the Maston home and exchanged warm-hearted greetings. In the sitting room, Maston sat in his usual easy chair. Helen Jean sat at the end of the couch nearest to him. The couch sits at an angle pointing slightly away from Maston's chair. Helen Jean turned herself toward Maston. Stan chose to sit on the floor, so he might face the elderly gentlemen directly. He was eager to listen and not miss a word.

The conversation moved along familiar lines. Maston's gentle voice droned on as he shared some of his favorite anecdotes. He lifted most of the experiences out of his own lifetime repertoire. The monologue mesmerized Stan. His mother was too busy taking notes to come under the spell.

Eventually, Helen Jean sensed that their stay was beginning to tax Maston's strength. Discreetly, she took the first opportunity to conclude the briefing. The pair excused themselves and left.

While they drove away Stan responded to the experience. He declared to his mother:

> You know? I've heard you and Dad talk about Dr. Maston over these years. . . . Today the thought crossed my mind of the Scripture talking about sitting at the feet of the prophets. . . . I really felt that I was sitting at the feet of a great man of God today.

Randall is the oldest son of the Parkses. While his brothers aspire to be missionaries, Randall already serves with the Foreign Mission Board in Egypt. During his seminary studies at Southwestern he became acquainted with Maston as the grand, old professor on campus.

Once the archives department of the seminary's library presented a special display of Maston memorabilia. While viewing the display, Randall read some hate mail Maston had received years before. It was during the period that Maston was the staunch protagonist of the black cause among Southern Baptists. It impressed Randall that Maston held no rancor in his heart. He showed no evidence of cynicism.

A second impression that Randall gained about Maston was that the aging professor had not grown stale with his accumulation of knowledge. He continued to learn and expand his mind.

Maston's impact on the three sons of Keith Parks indicates the durability of his memory among Southern Baptists. There are still many young adults whose lives he has touched. It holds the promise that Maston's significance

will linger for a long time. The rising generation of journeymen and second-generation missionaries guarantee it.

Jack Glaze is a former missionary to Argentina. He is
currently professor of missions at the New Orleans Baptist
Seminary. He came under the influence of Maston first
through missionary colleagues who studied with Maston.
Later during Maston's visits to South America he impressed Glaze directly with his personality and his ideas.

Once when Glaze was alone with Maston they discussed at length some of the crucial issues in missions.
Maston's emphasis on the primacy of biblical principles as
the basis for methodology proved especially helpful to the
missionary. He looked directly at the professor and said,
"I have never been a student of yours, but from now on
I want to be counted as your disciple." Maston humbly
consented.

During his last furlough in 1983, Glaze experienced
more culture shock than ever before. He had served for
thirty years as a missionary. On previous furloughs he was
somewhat aware of the erosion of morals in American
Christianity. On this occasion, however, Glaze was jolted
to the core. It concerned him so deeply that he wrote out
his troubled thoughts for possible future reference.

Not long after Glaze read an article by Maston in a
Baptist periodical. It astounded Glaze how coincidental
his thinking was to Maston's expressed concerns. Maston
lamented the shift from the biblical ideal of serving persons to a more crass professionalism in the churches. It
prompted Glaze to retrieve his notes from the file cabinet.
The parallelism of his own musings with Maston's article

stunned him. He wrote at the bottom of his notes, "I *am* a disciple of Maston!"

Jack Glaze and Justice Anderson have at least two notable things in common. They were colleagues together in the International Baptist Theological Seminary in Buenos Aires. They are also contemporary professors of missions in two of the Southern Baptist Seminaries: New Orleans and Southwestern, respectively.

It is a point of interest that Maston has strongly influenced four professors of missions in four of the six Southern Baptist theological institutions. In addition to the two above-mentioned men, there is Alan Neely at Southeastern, and Francis DuBose at Golden Gate.

Anderson sketches an account to help given by Maston that obviously had divine timing. The Foreign Mission Board offered Anderson a position with the headquarters staff in 1980. The invitation carried an impressive challenge. Anderson pondered the decision for a long time. His teaching ministry at Southwestern was beginning to open up for him in several exciting directions. Anderson and his wife had talked at great length. They had reached a standstill. They prayed earnestly for guidance. No sense of direction came.

Frustration set in. One day Anderson was sitting at his desk at the seminary. The quandary virtually immobilized him. He urgently felt the need to resolve the matter. Yet he could not determine what he should do. He was deep in thought when the telephone rang. Maston's soft voice interrupted Anderson's meditation, "This is T. B. Maston."

Anderson greeted him, "Hello, Dr. Maston. It's good to hear your voice."

"Well, Justice, I heard you are having to make a decision," Maston began.

Anderson thought to himself, *The grapevine is still working.* To his old professor, Anderson confirmed, "That's right. Mary Ann and I are having a very hard time deciding."

Maston continued, "I don't want to interfere at all, but I did want to share with you two things that might help you."

Maston proceeded to share two of his favorite personal anecdotes. One is about his time of decision some thirty years before when The Southern Baptist Theological Seminary in Louisville, Kentucky, invited Maston to teach. During his visit there he met W. O. Carver. Carver's counsel made an indelible impression on Maston. Maston has shared it in turn with students and colleagues many times. Carver said, "After you have thought through a thing from every possible viewpoint, if your head tells you one thing and your heart tells you something else, you had better follow your heart."

The other incident relates to Maston's earlier years as a professor. Some friends had urged him to consider teaching on the college level instead of in a seminary. In discussing the matter with L. R. Scarborough, president of Southwestern, a quotation from B. H. Carroll surfaced. Scarborough quoted his predecessor's words, "If you definitely feel that the Lord has led you here, then the burden of proof should be that you leave."

Anderson listened as in a trance.
Maston went on,

Those two counsels have been a great help to me in major
decisions I've faced. Think now, if the Lord brought you
here, have you been able to finish what the Lord wanted
you to do here? And, second, if it's between your head and
your heart, you better go with your heart.

Anderson heartily thanked Maston for his counsel. The
conversation ended. As Anderson replaced the phone re-
ceiver, an awesome sense of resolution washed over him.
He sensed with clarity the right decision. They would stay.
That's what his heart was telling him. That's what the
Lord intended. His emotions erupted. Tears flowed! He
wept in relief and gratitude.

Later the same day, Anderson sought for Maston. He
found him in his study carrel. Anderson poked his head
in the partly opened doorway. "Dr. Maston," he confided,
"I just wanted to tell you how much I appreciate the little
phone call. It wasn't you, it wasn't your word, but the
Lord used you to help me make a very important decision."

In the Latin American scene Maston holds more sway
than any other Protestant theologian in the realm of
Christian ethics. Edgar Hallock suggests that his popularity and impact are as substantial among Latin American
Baptists as among Southern Baptists. Maston's extensive
travels undoubtedly account for this renown. However,
his last journey in that direction was to Central American
and Mexico in 1970.

There is a more durable factor contributing to Maston's reputation in Latin America. Translations of his books in the Latin American languages explain his popularity more than his travels. Of his twenty-four published titles, four appear in Spanish translations and four in Portuguese. They enjoy a wide distribution throughout the continent.

On March 13, 1987, Maston was the featured speaker for chapel at Southwestern Seminary. The black students of the National Baptist Student Fellowship wanted him to represent them. The vice-president of the organization, Kevin Hardwick, introduced him. Hardwick's words were significant to this story because he referred to Maston's missionary journeys to Latin America.

Hardwick began with the rhetorical question, "What manner of man is this?" As he continued, Maston bowed his head: "What manner of man can travel throughout this country and throughout Central and South America? And can carry the gospel so forcefully? . . . Dr. Thomas Buford Maston is a kind man . . . a warm man . . . we take great pleasure in presenting to you today . . ."

It is customary for Maston to awaken very early in the morning. On such occasions he lies in bed thinking. He prays and reflects on the goodness of God in those solitary hours. On September 13, 1985, he shared with the author that he had awakened around three or four in the morning. His thoughts focused on "how grateful I am for how the Lord has blessed my life."

Maston lives his days in gratitude. He thanks God for his family. With all of the trials and heartaches, he is thankful for both of his sons for who they are. He is grateful for Mommie—oh so grateful. "Thank you, Mommie, for what you have done and do for me and for what you have meant and mean to me."Again, Maston prays, "Thank you, Father, for bringing Mommie into my life and permitting us to walk life's pathways together all these years."

There are poignant words in the poem Tom Maston wrote when he proposed to Essie Mae. After she consented he added a final stanza:

> Lord, Thou hast heard the answer she made.
> When our lives come to an end,
> And we to heaven and to You ascend,
> May we always Thy will have obeyed
> And may we, Dear Lord, hear Thee say,
> Well done, you two, Tom and Essie Mae.

Notwithstanding Maston's morning reveries of gratitude, he is not yet ready to resign from servanthood. There is the matter of God's unfinished will.

On November 9, 1985, Maston said,

I'm about to finish the manuscript I'm working on . . . Early this morning I woke up and began to think about what I'm going to do next. I just can't sit down and do nothing. If I do, I'm through.

"They shall mount up with wings as eagles . . . run, and not be weary . . . walk, and not faint."
And he shall sit and not quit.

The servant-pilgrim holds a valid passport. His visa extends.

Appendix: Maston's Published Books

The Bible and Family Relations. Nashville: Broadman, 1983. (coauthored with William M. Tillman, Jr.)

The Bible and Race. Nashville: Broadman, 1959.

Biblical Ethics: A Biblical Survey. Cleveland: World Publishing Co., 1967. (republished Waco, TX: Word Books, 1969 and reprinted *Biblical Ethics — A Survey: A Guide To the Ethical Message of the Scriptures From Genesis Through Revelation.* Mercer University Press, 1982)

The Christian and Race Relations. Memphis, TN: Brotherhood Commission, SBC, n.d.

The Christian, The Church, and Contemporary Problems. Waco, TX: Word Books, 1968.

The Christian in the Modern World. Nashville: Broadman, 1952.

Christian Principles and Contemporary Social Problems. Fort Worth, TX: Privately published, n.d.

Christianity and World Issues. New York: Macmillan, 1957.

The Conscience of A Christian. Waco, TX: Word Books, 1971.

The Ethic of the Christian Life. Hogg, Gayle, ed. (Religious Education Series), El Paso: Casa Bautista, 1982.

God Speaks Through Suffering. Waco, TX: Word Books, 1977.

God's Will: A Dynamic Discovery. Nashville: Convention Press, 1987, revised edition of *God's Will and Your Life.*

God's Will and Your Life. Nashville: Broadman, 1964.

Handbook For Church Recreation Leaders. Nashville: The Sunday School Board, SBC, 1937.

How To Face Grief. Waco, TX: Word Books, 1978.

Isaac Backus: Pioneer of Religious Liberty. London: James Clark & Co., 1962.

"Mommie": A personal Tribute to Essie Mae (Mrs. T. B.) Maston. Fort Worth, TX: Privately published, 1980.

Of One. Atlanta: Home Mission Board, SBC, 1946.

Real Life In Christ. Nashville: Broadman, 1974.

Right or Wrong? Nashville: Broadman, 1955. (revised with William M. Pinson Jr., coauthor, 1971)

Segregation and Desegregation: A Christian Approach. New York: MacMillan, 1959.

Suffering: A Personal Perspective. Nashville: Broadman, 1967.

To Walk As He Walked. Nashville: Broadman, 1985.

Treasures from Holy Scripture. Nashville: Broadman Press, 1987.

Why Live the Christian Life? Nashville: Broadman, 1974 and Nashville: Nelson, 1974.

Words of Wisdom. Nashville: Broadman, 1984.

A World In Travail. Nashville: Broadman, 1954.

Appendix: Published Translations of Maston's Works

Benar Atau Salah. Condensed Indonesian translation of *Right Or Wrong,* Bandung: Geredja Baptis, 1958.

Bueno O Malo? Spanish translation of *Right Or Wrong?* by Hiram Duffer, El Paso: Casa Bautista, 1957

Bueno O Malo? Spanish translation of revised 1971 ed. of *Right or Wrong?* co-authored with William M. Pinson, translation by Ruben Zorzoli and Alicia de Zorzoli, El Paso: Casa Bautista de Publicaciones, 1975.

Certo Ou Errado. Portugese translation of *Right Or Wrong?* by J. Reis Pereira, Rio: Casa Publicadora Batista, 1958.

Cristianismo e Problemas Mundiais. Portuguese translation of *Christianity and World Issues,* no publ. data.

Consejos A La Juventud. Spanish translation of Maston's notes. The title means "Advice for Youth," by Hiram F. Duffer, Jr., El Paso: Casa Bautista, n.d.

Etica De La Vida Cristiana Sus Principios Basicos. Spanish translation of *Why Live the Christian Life?* by Floreal Ureta, Buenos Aires: Casa Bautista, 1981.

Etica del Cristiano en el Mundo en Crisis. Spanish translation by Bob Adams. The title means "Christian Ethics In a World in Crisis," El Paso: Casa Bautista, n.d.

Gottes Wille: Antworten Auf Fragen Junger Menschen. German translation of *God's Will and Your Life,* [translator not given] Kassel: J. G. Onchen, 1968.

A Igreja e o Mundo. Portuguese translation of some of Maston's notes. The title means "The Church and the World," no publ. data.

Kehendak Allah. Indonesian translation of *God's Will and Your Life,* [translator not given] Semarang: Seminari Theologia Baptist, 1970.

Manual para la Direccion de las Actividades Recreatives de la Iglesia. Spanish translation of *Handbook For Church Recreation Leaders* by Viola Campbell, El Paso: Casa Bautista, 1951

[*Right Or Wrong?* — Arabic script]. Arabic translation by Jereyes Del'Leh, Beirut: Baptist Publishing House, 1955.

A Vontade De Deus E Sua Vida. Portuguese translation of *God's Will and Your Life* by Thurmon Bryant, 2nd ed., Brazil: J.U.E.R.P., 1979.